This Book Is Free and Yours to Keep

THIS BOOK IS FREE AND YOURS TO KEEP

NOTES FROM THE APPALACHIAN PRISON BOOK PROJECT

EDITED BY CONNIE BANTA, KRISTIN DEVAULT-JUELFS, DESTINEE HARPER, KATY RYAN, AND ELLEN SKIRVIN

 West Virginia University Press • Morgantown

All royalties from this publication will go to the
Appalachian Prison Book Project.

First edition published 2024 by West Virginia University Press
Printed in the United States of America
ISBN 978-1-959000-35-8 (paperback)
ISBN 978-1-959000-36-5 (ebook)

Library of Congress Cataloging-in-Publication Data
Names: Banta, Connie, 1952- editor. | DeVault-Juelfs, Kristin, 1997- editor.
| Harper, Destinee, 1999- editor. | Ryan, Katy, 1968- editor.
| Skirvin, Ellen, 1992- editor.
Title: This book is free and yours to keep : notes from the Appalachian Prison
Book Project / Connie Banta, Kristin DeVault-Juelfs, Destinee Harper, Katy
Ryan, Ellen Skirvin. Description: Morgantown : West Virginia University
Press, [2024] | Includes bibliographical references.
Identifiers: LCCN 2024009309
| ISBN 9781959000358 (paperback) | ISBN 9781959000365 (ebook)
Subjects: LCSH: Appalachian Prison Book Project. | Prisoners—Books
and Reading—Appalachian Region. | Prisoners as authors—Appalachian
Region. | Prisoners—Education—Appalachian Region. | Book Donations—
Appalachian Region. | LCGFT: Essays. | Personal correspondence.
| Drawings. Classification: LCC Z1039.P83 T48 2024
| DDC 365/.66--dc23/eng/20240710
LC record available at https://lccn.loc.gov/2024009309

Book and cover design by Than Saffel / WVU Press

To Darrin Lester, our friend

Mountain Peaks! Jagged Edg
peaks! Rocky Terrain as
our Pain! Reading Betwee
Story, while Being trapp
Go Insane! Trying 2 RE
Past, So That "Hour" Presenc
Be Bright Like the Son, A
Even with The Strain, We
Book, Until we finish the
I= A Great Stage Tha
A Place 2 Unleash My Fru
age! EyE Read 2 Calm My N
after EyE Have Had a
ith all of my Bad Daz

CONTENTS

PREFACE

Hugh Williams, Jr.

There was once a time when the thought of spending months in a closet-sized room with no one to talk to would have terrified me, possibly even drove me crazy. But that was seventeen years ago.

I was arrested at seventeen and given a fifty-year sentence. Now I have spent seventeen years, half of my life, in prison, and once again, I find myself in solitary confinement. I am in my eighth month of solitary confinement, and I've only been out of my cell once in the last two-and-a-half months. Where once I would have been driven mad, now I find the peace, quiet, and solitude to be comforting. Sometimes I go weeks without speaking.

With all the chaos and stress that can become one's daily life in prison, solitude can be preferred over being involved with other people's drama and problems.

My point is that life in prison can be traumatic and life-altering whether one is by oneself or around other people, and it can have negative side effects no matter who you are or where you are. Like an animal who suffers continuous abuse, we can find ourselves becoming withdrawn and antisocial and feeling as if we are alone in this world with no one to care whether we wake up in the morning. I've lived feeling like that, and it is the loneliest feeling. Never have I felt so alone and helpless, a creature in exile and lost with no friends or family to ease the pain and bitterness that grows wild in the uncultivated heart.

Fortunately, I was to receive a blessing that helped open my heart, enlighten my mind, and allow me to thrive, no matter where the winds would take me.

When I was locked away, I was a high school dropout. Yet, even before that, my education was stalled. I could only add and subtract when it came to math, and all I knew of science was the process of photosynthesis (and literally *nothing* else). Of history, I could only tell you the most basic facts that anyone familiar with American culture could tell you, and I could only read at a third- or fourth-grade level. I couldn't tell you what a noun, verb, or sentence was. Suddenly I found myself in chains, locked in a cage, and exiled from my homeland and all I held dear for a sentence of fifty years, a debt that I am still uncertain that I will ever live to see paid. Hope for me to grow was in short supply.

Every teacher I had ever known had given up on me when I was free. Who would teach me now that I was in chains?

Before my incarceration, I had never read a book that was more than fifteen or twenty pages. It never held my interest; in fact, I hated to read. I spent weeks in a cell in solitary confinement simply staring at the walls, growing more hopeless and depressed with each day. Indeed, I learned that the world still turned without me, and I was soon forgotten.

Growing up, I always saw my Aunt Teresa reading whenever she wasn't working and had a moment to spare. I once asked her why she read so much, and she smiled at me as though she knew a great secret. She told me that by reading a book, if the story was good, it could take you to other worlds and teach you things you never thought were possible. I thought she'd gone insane. How could ink on paper create a world? Years later, locked in a tiny, cold room covered in graffiti, curse words, and racist slurs, I'd sit on a very thin mat on a steel bunk jutting out of a wall, and desperate (near suicide), I would learn the secret Aunt Teresa knew about books and reading. It would save my life.

I learned that reading not only takes you to other worlds, but when given good books and well-crafted stories, I could leave the cell that bound and limited my body and held me captive and alone. I gained new perspectives; I was given new friends—friends that did not abandon me or forget me. Together, we traveled places, sailed seas, fought wars. We sought redemption from our past and struggled to become better men, and in time, we found forgiveness, and perhaps I found a place or two where even someone like me could be called a hero. And no one laughed when it was said.

For most people, this is a very big world that is wide and reaches farther than they can see, and that is good. Yet it is not so for me. Physically, I traverse my world in less than ten strides. Yet, with every book I have the honor to read, I leave this place, meet new people, learn new things, and in some way become a better man. I wanted to be like these good men and women who didn't let mistakes or their past crimes stop them from seeking redemption or stop them from doing what is hard or right. Yes, to some these are just books, and on their pages are simply stories, but to a teenager who just turned eighteen and stepped off a prison bus at Brushy Mountain State Penitentiary (in 2005 before the infamous prison was closed and made a tourist attraction), many of these books' heroes and struggling characters influenced my still-developing mind and provided me with an outlet to freedom, hope when I had no hope, and a role model to encourage me when I had no good role models. Having access to books literally saved my life.

With encouragement to do right and become better, books made me strive to earn my GED in 2007 and take college courses. I began reading fiction, and as I read and became better at reading and writing, I wrote a book of poetry. Then I moved to nonfiction books on history and philosophy, then to books on psychology and on different religions, and even some books on the conditions of society and crime.

I was the one all my teachers gave up on, but ten years later I became a teacher. I taught GED classes, a class on career management, and a class on history. And it all began with a shivering boy, alone and crying in a cell, wanting to die when he was handed a book of fiction by John Sanford about a detective named Lucas Davenport. I still can't believe the difference a book can make. There are endless possibilities.

And so, programs like the Appalachian Prison Book Project that work to give people in prison access to books are not only changing lives but *saving* lives—creating writers, teachers, lovers of literature and art—by simply giving a book with a kindly written letter, personally signed "Emily,"[1] that brings light to a dark place and shows someone that someone else does care and that the world is not so dark and we are not so alone.

Indeed, there are many worlds that await and many chains to be broken.

Having received such secrets and blessings, I am humbled in an ocean of gratitude, and all I can say is thank you, though I know it will never be enough to repay you for all that you have given to me.

Notes

1   Hugh Williams, Jr. received a book from one of our volunteers, Emily. At the end of this essay, he asked that "the other workers who kindly send the materials and sign their names" also be recognized. If you have ever volunteered at APBP, here is a note from him: "All of you are very much appreciated and once again I send my thanks."

INTRODUCTION

Katy Ryan

*A*bout 200 letters arrive at the Appalachian Prison Book Project (APBP) every week from people in confinement who are looking for something to read. The requests cover the spectrum: sci-fi, westerns, poetry, manga, astronomy, LGBTQ+ literature, books by Black writers, books on how to draw or learn music or start a business, books on indigenous histories, dictionaries, books in Spanish, puzzle books. One person only wanted books on West Virginia. Another wrote, "I'll read anything you send to me."

In response to these requests, APBP has mailed more than 70,000 free books to people imprisoned in six states: West Virginia, Virginia, Tennessee, Kentucky, Ohio, and Maryland. We have accumulated an archive of tens of thousands of letters that document reading practices and everyday life in prisons and jails in the early twenty-first century. These materials are a testament to the ways people held captive in our region continue to learn, to grow, and to support one another and their loved ones.

I know it's pretty much impossible to know everything, but I can't help but want to know everything.

—C. S. Mars

People also send artwork—sketches on envelopes, colored pencil drawings, watercolors, a gift to whoever opens the mail that day. You're sorting through a stack of envelopes, and suddenly there is a hummingbird, a mountain stream, SpongeBob SquarePants.

The letters we open literally move us—into prisons and organizing, into law schools and libraries, into policy and history. Since 2004, APBP has grown from a few dedicated students into a regional leader in the movement for educational justice. In addition to mailing books, APBP creates book clubs in prisons, pays tuition costs for students taking West Virginia University (WVU) courses in prison, and awards scholarships to released people enrolled in a college or university in our state. APBP also engages the public in conversations about the prison industrial complex and transformative justice. Central to everything we do is the belief that education is a human right and that building community is essential to social change.

The History

> I believe in sunshine.
> In windmills and waterfalls,
> tricycles and rocking chairs.
> And i believe that seeds grow into sprouts.
> And sprouts grow into trees.
>
> —*Assata Shakur*[1]

APBP grew out of a 2004 graduate class I taught at WVU on the history and literature of imprisonment in the United States. As students read stories, memoirs, and poetry by people in prison, they were struck by the many references to reading: Malcolm X studying

Envelope art by Brenda Brown (top) Envelope art by O. Ogun (bottom)

the dictionary; Jimmy Santiago Baca stealing a textbook and falling in love with Wordsworth; Assata Shakur sustained by the company of literature: "Me and James Baldwin are communicating. His fiction is more real than this reality."[2] The students in my English class were inclined toward the liberating capacity of reading and writing, but in the context of literal imprisonment, their understanding became more potent and their desire to take action more urgent.

When we learned there were no organizations providing free books to people in prison in our state and few in our region, we decided to create one. Joined by university and community members, we spent two years collecting paperbacks and raising money. We held bake sales and book sales. Musicians played fundraising concerts. We left collection jars at local businesses. More than once in our early years, we ran out of money for postage. Our donated workspace is a beloved room filled with books in the historic Aull Center, a branch of the Morgantown Public Library.

In 2012, with help from the WVU Entrepreneurial Law Clinic and guided by the caution in INCITE!'s 2007 *The Revolution Will Not Be Funded: Beyond the Non-Profit Industrial Complex*, APBP became a 501c3 nonprofit.[3] APBP remains a volunteer-driven organization funded entirely by individual donations and small grants.

Beyond responding to letters, we knew we wanted to work directly with people in prison and also knew we had a lot to learn. In April 2014, we organized the Educational Justice & Appalachian Prisons Symposium, with support from the West Virginia Humanities Council. This three-day event gathered 200 educators, activists, artists, lawyers, prison staff, and administrators. The opening panel featured three incarcerated men who discussed their experiences with education. Keynote speakers were Rebecca Ginsburg, director of the Education Justice Project; Kyes Stevens, director of the Alabama Prison Creative Arts + Education Project; and R. Dwayne Betts, poet, lawyer, and (now) director of Freedom Reads. The momentum from this event led APBP in new directions.

Beginning in 2014, we began to create book clubs in prisons and developed a practice that continues to evolve. Reading and writing groups meet every other week and typically consist of fifteen inside members and three to five outside members. We have held book clubs at state and federal prisons for men and women, our conversations deepened by nonbinary, trans, and genderqueer members. The group decides together on what to read. Discussions are expansive, full of humor and insight—"circled up and thoughtful," in the words of Celeste Monet Blair, a founding inside member whose beautiful essay "The Power In Passing It On" appears in chapter four.[4]

Reading with people in prison strengthened our resolve to increase educational access and equity. In 2019, APBP worked with WVU to create credit-bearing college classes in prison and launched a fundraising campaign to cover costs for tuition and books. Two years later, Rayna Momen and I cofounded the WVU Higher Education in Prison Initiative, and WVU began to offer classes toward an associate degree program at a maximum-security prison.

People in prisons and jails overwhelmingly come from communities that have been excluded from higher education. Their participation in college classes and program design can bring their knowledge and experiences to bear on institutional policies and practices. Part of the promise of college-in-prisons programs is the transformation of higher education itself. Drawing from Dylan

Rodriguez and Buzz Alexander, Rachel Boccio writes that a limitation of even the best prison pedagogy "may be the faith it puts in the liberal bourgeois class (the activist scholar or the prison educator) to teach the captive class into freedom."[5] A narrow focus on educators going into prisons overlooks the leadership of incarcerated people who are there, already doing the work, and who show up, over and over and in so many ways. As Ya'iyr writes in his extraordinary poem "bioluminescence," included in chapter four, "some organisms that grow in darkness make their own light."

We are committed to changing structures while we cocreate learning spaces. To go through prison gates is to know this truth from John Wideman: "Power was absurdly apportioned all on one side."[6] Toting in books for mothers who may have lost custody of their children. Analyzing an essay when it is not possible to name the fullness of the pain in the room. It can seem, as with mailing books, like never enough.

Our dream is not more books in confinement but an end to torture, not more programs in prisons and jails but an end to mass incarceration and perpetual punishment. Craig Elias, an exceptional educator and writer, named the element that keeps our work going: catalytic love. "It pumps blood to broken hands, healing and preparing us to continue the work. The only sane way to respond to love like this is to make it count."

The Letters

People write to APBP for many reasons. When I'm asked what people in prison want to read, I think of a woman in Tennessee hoping for the sky, C. S. Mars longing to know everything, someone sliding Dudley Randall's *The Black Poets* to a teenager in a cell—and Dwayne Betts opening the first page.[7] I think of how often we don't know what we want to read until we are reading it.

Some letters ask for information on health, the law, or life after release. Other people are writing on behalf of someone else who wants to learn to read. Horace Nunley thanked us for books that help prepare for what is "in store for us once we're back. . . . I educate myself with the political and historical books you send me. Knowledge will free me and help me to never return to a cell." Letter

If we could find a book on the sky for me, I would love it very much.

—TN

writers affirm reading's path to personal growth, to knowledge and freedom, variations on Frederick Douglass's complex account of literacy.[8] In a well-known passage in his autobiography, Malcolm X wrote that he never felt more free than when he began to read behind bars: "I knew right there in prison that reading had forever changed the course of my life. As I see it today, the ability to read awoke inside me a long dormant craving to be mentally alive."[9]

Many letters describe how books provide imaginative escape and respite from suffering as well as a way to engage with the present and the future. Greg Whittington, director of Criminal Justice Reform for the ACLU of West Virginia and director of the West Virginia Family of Convicted People, credits reading in prison with reorienting his life.

> I would not be here today if people like yourself had not donated books to prison. I read at a third-grade level when I went in, and because of books that were provided by APBP, I read over a thousand books prior to my release. I could not wait to get back to my cell and see what the next chapter held for me! I escaped prison every day and traveled with Tom Sawyer, Lewis and Clark, Dante, and I traveled with folks in *The Canterbury Tales*. Little by little I became immersed in literature, and I escaped the violence and hate that was prison and began to transform myself into something more than a number.

It is not uncommon in English departments to find older literature anthologies abandoned in hallways or serving as doorstops. Writers to APBP tell us how valuable these resources are.

I was really surprised to receive the last book you sent me, the *Norton Anthology of American Literature*, Volume 2. It will definitely be an asset when I start the fall semester in August. That book is *the best* book that I've received in all 5 years of my time here. . . . I'll treasure it for many years to come.

You folks are doing a good thing with your program and even though you might not see first-hand evidence of it, what you do has a positive effect on a lot of lives! I want to thank you for the last book that you sent me: John Milton's "Paradise Lost." I have tried for over three years to obtain a copy and had almost given up on being able to find one.[10]

Reading can transport us to unfamiliar worlds and clarify the one we're in. In an essay on becoming a writer in prison, Steve Champion recounts how he and Stanley Tookie Williams began to study together at San Quentin and how a global picture came into view.

The books exposed our minds to countries, continents, and histories we had no idea existed. Slowly we began to develop a global picture. We began to see the links in human history, culture, and religion. We were starting to think critically without even realizing it. In a very real sense we became each other's student and teacher.[11]

And sometimes a book opens a literal door. Travis Norwood told us:

Because of your book program sending me Michie's *West Virginia Code Annotated*, I was able to litigate an amended sentence order from life without parole to eligibility for parole after serving 15 years. In other words, you helped save my life.

We know we don't always come through. Letters are lost, we're unable to find a good match, or a package arrives too late. Not everyone likes to read, not everyone can read. But prison book projects across the country are inundated with letters charged with the desire for books and for connection.

Many letters arrive like a flare, a meditation. And it matters that someone is listening. Ashley Van Natter wrote, "Even just writing to you guys makes this ole Mingo County boy's heart beat a little stronger." When we thanked Louie Whitecotton for sending his writing, he replied, "Whether my short essay ever gets included in your book, you have inspired me at the age of 65 years young to enlarge my territory and broaden my parameters." Another writer named Steven commented on the world of talent behind bars. He called it sad and shameful that "the general consensus is *not* geared toward learning, changing, overcoming, empowering. It just sucks something fierce." We agree. We reached out to ask if we could include his letter in this book. Our letter was returned with the word "deceased" stamped on the envelope.

This is the fear of so many: to die in prison.[12] We were able to locate Steven's father who gave us permission to include his son's words: "I think he would like that," he wrote. In his last letter to APBP, Steven practiced writing in Italian, thanked us for sending books "from the heart," and listed fifty-two titles he would like to read "in no particular order." Among them were Sun Tzu's *The Art of War,* Dante's *The Divine Comedy*, Philippe Aries's *The Hour of Our Death*, and Priscilla McMillan's *The Ruin of J. Robert Oppenheimer and the Birth of the Modern Arms Race*.

The letters and artwork in this collection work against what Patrick Elliot Alexander calls "voice dispossession." In his introduction to *From Slave Ship to Supermax,* Alexander reminds us that the experiences of incarcerated people are often sensationalized and distorted to fit the expectations of curious spectators or the genre conventions of confessional and redemption narratives. In contrast, Alexander argues, prison abuse narratives act as testimony and a call to action, "an account of utter defiance that illustrates how confined people resist authoritarian torment, reclaim their wounded bodies and psyches, establish desired community and political solidarity, and thereby undermine the asymmetries of power characteristic of carceral environments governed by a White supremacist disciplinary logic."[13] Alexander focuses on literary works by Toni Morrison, James Baldwin, Ernest J. Gaines, and Charles Johnson, but he acknowledges that, given the frequency with which people in prison endure physical and psychological harm, "*any* writing they produced from such a space could be termed a 'prisoner abuse narrative.'"[14] In their refusal to submit to an environment that often insists there is no meaningful present and no liberated future—only the unchangeable past—letter writers to APBP choose hope and tomorrow. They tell us what they want to read.

Our book aligns with a recent collection of essays by people involved with prison book projects across the country, *Books Through Bars: Stories from the Prison Books Movement* (2024), edited by Moira Marquis and Dave "Mac" Marquis. Two APBP volunteers, Ellen Skirvin and Valerie Surrett, contributed to this collection. *Books Through Bars* documents the history of a movement built by "regular people, without a lot of money and no powerful allies."[15] Our book also joins an epistolary tradition that brings personal letters into public view, a tradition that includes *Dear Books to Prisoners: Letters from the Incarcerated* as well as works by imprisoned people engaged in political struggle—for example, George Jackson's *Soledad, Brother*; Antonio Gramsci's *Letters from Prison*; Martin Luther King, Jr.'s "Letter from Birmingham Jail"; *The Letters of Joe Hill*; *The Prison Letters of Nelson Mandela*; *The Rosenberg Letters*; and Jack Henry Abbott's *In the Belly of the Beast*.[16] Angela Y. Davis begins *If They Come in the Morning: Voices of Resistance*—a collection of letters, essays, and poems—with an open letter James Baldwin wrote when she was in prison. Baldwin begins, as he often did, by seizing upon the history of the contemporary moment:

> One might have hoped that, by this hour, the very sight of chains on black flesh, or the very sight of chains, would be so intolerable a sight for the American people, and so unbearable a memory, that they would themselves spontaneously rise up and strike off the manacles.[17]

APBP is one of many organizations acting on what is intolerable and unbearable, against cages and chains, and we do this from a region that has been stigmatized and subjected to the environmental violence and extractive industries of racial capitalism, as discussed in chapter three.

Letters from people in confinement continue to fuel movement building. In 2017, the *Transgender Studies Quarterly* published letters by CeCe McDonald,[18] and in 2021, journalist Emily Bazelon launched the Prison Letters Project, a public database to amplify the voices of people in prison. In collaboration with John J. Lennon and the Law and Racial Justice Center at Yale, the project offers a way for lawyers, journalists, pen-pals, and others to offer assistance with legal cases.[19] The project has its origins in a 2019 letter Yutico Briley sent to Brazelon while he was incarcerated in Louisiana, asking for help with his innocence case. By sharing APBP letters and creative writing, we want more people to join in this work of reading, listening, and responding to people in prison and to participate in "grassroots planning"[20] and meaningful structural change.

The Learning

Our title, *This Book Is Free and Yours to Keep*, comes from the first line of the form letter we include in outgoing packages. When we composed that sentence two decades ago, we had no idea how radical it would become.

Like all prison book projects, APBP navigates a world of restrictions regarding mailing processes and book content.[21] We have a "no send" list with dozens of prisons and jails that only accept books from a distributor or publisher. Increasingly correspondence sent into prisons is digitally scanned and saved, available for information gathering.[22] Many prisons will not accept coloring books or composition notebooks or cards. Some reject packages with labels. Federal prisons require white-only packaging. Some prisons require preapproval forms. Some restrict the number of books a person can have. Some only allow book donations to be sent to the prison library, not to individuals.

This may sound corny but it is such a great, uplifting feeling to hear your name at mail-call and receive a package with a book that can take you beyond the bars and further than the stars.

—Jasop Rollins

Surveillance practices also make it difficult for people in prison, here and around the globe, to write and publish their writing. The memoir of Mohamedou Ould Slahi, who was detained for fourteen years without charge at Guantánamo, contained over 2,500 redactions when it was first published in 2015. The unredacted version of *Guantánamo Diary* was published in 2022. Some of the writing in *Poems from Guantánamo: The Detainees Speak* (2007), edited by Marc Falkoff, was initially etched in Styrofoam cups by writers who did not have pen or paper. The Pentagon reviewed every poem and rejected most.[23] Behrouz Boochani had to send his memoir *No Friend but the Mountains: Writing from Manus Prison* (2018) out by text message.

Working on this book, we worried every time we sent an update to contributors that it might prompt unfavorable attention from officials. We have omitted most of the names and identifying information of specific prisons as well as references to individual cases. We are always concerned that our work might cause harm, and we realize we might never know. It is difficult to not suspect that the acceleration of book bans and mail scanning practices are reactions to the capacity of literature and letters to connect and mobilize people. The real contraband is, as Kaia Stern suggests in the context of college-in-prison programs, human connection.[24]

The education that happens through APBP moves in multiple directions. Volunteers become inspired to learn why the United States incarcerates so many people and what needs to change.[25] A former graduate intern Maggie Montague listed on the APBP blog eleven things she learned from reading letters. Here is the fifth:

"People disappear too easily."[26] We have an abolition working group that has hosted online book discussions of Mariame Kaba's *We Do This 'Til We Free Us: Abolitionist Organizing and Transforming Justice* and Angela Y. Davis, Gina Dent, Erica R. Meiners, and Beth E. Richie's *Abolition. Feminism. Now.*[27] In 2023, we partnered with Working Films to screen five abolitionist short films.

We've learned how important it is to develop partnerships, to collaborate, and to cultivate the courage to learn in public. We are honored to be part of a national alliance of prison book projects that shares information and resources.[28] We are a member of a statewide coalition of organizations dedicated to ending overreliance on policing and prisons. Sylvia Ryerson visited WVU in 2017 to discuss the phenomenal work of Appalshop and the radio station WMMT. The program "Calls from Home" records messages from friends and family to their loved ones in prison and broadcasts the messages over the airways. For over fifteen years, "Calls from Home" has offset the costs of phone calls, helped families and friends stay connected, and contributed to decarceration and abolition efforts. A new documentary film tells the story of the radio show from the perspective of those most impacted by incarceration.

Supporters from across the country and as far as Japan and Ghana find their way to APBP. In 2021, Lisa Reedy wrote, "I placed an order of books to be sent to your project as a gift to honor my friend Shawntel Enmsinger, who just passed from a long battle with cancer. She was a librarian and a passionate humanitarian, and one of her last Facebook posts was asking for people to donate to your project." Around the same time, a postcard arrived "from an old Tennessee Hillbilly now living in the desert," who told us, "Having grown up in the Appalachian foothills, I know it's needed there so much. Keep fighting the good fight. Don't know shit about manga—hope these work."[29]

Our grounding in West Virginia has deepened our intersectional understanding of how dispossession, racism, poverty, gender-based violence, transphobia, and other systemic forces reproduce inequity and injustice and drive incarceration. In West Virginia, like most states, Black people are disproportionately arrested, convicted, and sentenced to prison.[30] Appalachia is often depicted as a homogenous white geographical space, a characterization that obscures significant Black populations in the region as well as Appalachian history, which includes periods with major multiracial movements in and out of the region.[31] In 2021, Crystal Good launched *Black By God*, West Virginia's only Black newspaper, to advance a more accurate understanding of race in Appalachia and to center the voices of Black Appalachians.[32]

The scale of the carceral regime also means millions of white people, overwhelmingly poor, are caught in this massive and traumatizing system that, at enormous cost, returns people over and over to cages. LGBTQ+ people, poor people, people with mental illnesses, people with histories of trauma and addiction, and survivors of intimate partner violence are especially vulnerable to criminal punishment.[33]

The criminalization of addiction and poverty hits hard and at home. In recent decades, central Appalachia has become one of the most concentrated sites for prison building in the country, as Judah Schept reports in *Coal, Cages, Crisis: The Rise of the Prison*

Economy in Central Appalachia. Prisons in our region are often unreachable by public transportation, located on former mining sites, unsafe for those who work and live inside. Prisons are built on toxic lands that "constantly expose those inside to serious environmental hazards, from tainted water to harmful air pollutants. These conditions manifest in health conditions and deaths that are unmistakably linked to those hazards."[34] And the economic promises that accompany prison siting are mostly unrealized.[35] Rather than regenerative economic models, we are given punishment and prison, which, as Betts writes, "ruins everyone: prisoners, guards, family, the ground it's built on."[36]

The criminal legal system also fails to provide lasting relief or safety to victims of violence and harm. More than half of the survivors of serious violence, Danielle Sered stresses in *Until We Reckon*, choose not to report what has happened to them. They "prefer *nothing* to everything available to them through law enforcement."[37] There is, for us, no contradiction between dismantling systems of harm and supporting survivors of abuse and violence and those who have had a loved one hurt or killed. Many people in prison are survivors; many APBP volunteers are survivors. We understand our work as part of the larger movement to repair the intergenerational harm caused by white supremacy and systemic dispossession.

We did not set out to build a community; the work required it. Rayna Momen put it this way: "What I know is that I've never loved an organization more wholly or given my time more freely; it means that much to be part of something so beautiful." We are learning to move "at the speed of relationships." "At the speed of trust."[38]

Art by Liz Pavlovic,
local Morgantown artist

Words Just Kept

*Things don't fall apart. Things
hold. Lines connect in thin ways
that last and last and lines become
generations made out of pictures
and words just kept.*

—Lucille Clifton[39]

In the following editorial statement, we explain our process for selecting materials and securing permissions from over seventy contributors. Chapter one, "Book Requests," contains excerpts from letters that illustrate a range of reading interests and practices. Chapter two, "Access and Restrictions," reviews obstacles that people in prison encounter when trying to obtain information, books, and other resources. Chapter three, "Letters as Windows," includes communication about matters beyond books: solitary confinement, separation from families and friends, being young and in prison, life in Appalachia, physical and mental health, and future plans. Chapter four, "Circles, Classes, Conversations," features creative work and reflections from APBP book clubs and WVU classes. In chapter five, "Weaving Webs," we describe how the exchange of books and ideas deepens connections among people in prison and among volunteers and how it can help to bridge the divide of prison walls.

Our collection concludes with an essay by Steven Lazar who had a 1.8 percent chance of not dying in prison. He made the calculation that he would die "a miserable, sad, and painful death surrounded by steel, concrete, and clatter, instead of children, grandchildren, and love." Yet, in 2023, Steven walked out of prison, exonerated. He read this book manuscript as a free person in Philadelphia. I spoke to him on the phone a week after his release, and I will not forget the way he spoke the names of friends still locked up. Their confinement was, he said, unacceptable. Doing this work constantly recalls me to the end of Gwendolyn Brooks's poem "Paul Robeson."

> we are each other's
> harvest:
> we are each other's
> business:
> we are each other's
> magnitude and bond.[40]

We wish we could share with you the texture of handwritten letters, the healing energy of the Aull Center, the feel and smell of perfectly used books. In the introduction to Austin Reed's *The Life and the Adventures of a Haunted Convict*, the earliest known U.S. prison autobiography,

Caleb Smith reflects on the process of transcription: "Compare the photograph of a manuscript page to a transcription of the same, and you can see, right away, how much has been lost."[41] Despite what has been lost in transcription, despite all we could not include, we hope this collection communicates something of the urgency, political education, determination, humor, compassion, grief, sorrow, and wisdom that arrives every day in the APBP post office box.

Notes

1   Assata Shakur, *Assata: An Autobiography* (Chicago: Lawrence Hill Books, 2001), 1.

2   Malcolm X, *The Autobiography of Malcolm X* (New York: Ballantine, 2015), 176, 182; Jimmy Santiago Baca, "Coming Into Language," in *Doing Time: 25 Years of Prison Writing* (New York: Arcade, 2011), 102; Assata Shakur, *Assata: An Autobiography* (Chicago: Lawrence Hill Books, 2001), 155.

3   INCITE, ed., *The Revolution Will Not Be Funded: Beyond the Non-Profit Industrial Complex* (Durham: Duke University Press, 2017).

4   For more on APBP book clubs, see Katy Ryan, Valerie Surrett, and Rayna Momen, "Reading and Writing between the Devil and the Deep Blue," in *Teaching Literature and Writing in Prisons,* eds. Sheila Smith McCoy and Patrick Elliot Alexander (New York: Modern Language Association, 2023), 231–44.

5   Rachel Boccio, "Toward the Soul of a Transformational Praxis: Close Reading and the Liberationist Possibilities of Prison Education," *Pedagogy* 17, no. 3 (October 2017): 429.

6   John Wideman, *Brothers and Keepers* (New York: Mariner Books, 2005), 84.

7   Reginald Dwayne Betts, "We Must Give All Prisoners Access to Resources to Pursue College Education," *Time,* May 27, 2021, https://time.com/6052113 /prisoners-college-education/. Also see Betts, *A Question of Freedom* (New York: Penguin, 2010), 164.

8   Frederick Douglass, *Narrative of the Life of Frederick Douglass: An American Slave, Written by Himself*, edited by John R. McKivigan, Peter P. Hinks, and Heather L. Kaufman (New Haven: Yale University Press, 2001), 34–39.

9   Malcolm X, *The Autobiography of Malcolm X* (New York: Ballantine Books, 1992), 206.

10   These quotations were saved and shared by volunteers in our early years without the names of letter writers.

11   Steve Champion, "On Connection and Collaboration: Becoming a Writer in Prison," in *Demands of the Dead: Executions, Activism, and Storytelling in the United States*, ed. Katy Ryan (Iowa City: University of Iowa Press, 2012), 61.

12   The UCLA School of Law Behind Bars Data Project, launched in March 2020 during Covid, now tracks all causes of death in state and federal prisons and is the only nationwide accounting of deaths in custody. Michael Everett and Lauren Woyczynski, "UCLA Law Releases New Database to Monitor Deaths in U.S. Prisons," *UCLA Covid Behind Bars,* accessed May 2024, https://uclacovidbehindbars.org/intro-carceral-mortality.

13   Patrick Elliot Alexander, *From Slave Ship to Supermax: Mass Incarceration, Prisoner Abuse, and the New Neo-Slave Narrative* (Philadelphia: Temple University Press, 2017), 15.

14   Patrick Elliot Alexander, *From Slave Ship to Supermax: Mass Incarceration, Prisoner Abuse, and the New Neo-Slave Narrative* (Philadelphia: Temple University Press, 2017), 14.

15   *Books Beyond Bars: Stories from the Prison Books Movement*, eds. Moira Marquis and Dave "Mac" Marquis (Athens: University of Georgia Press, 2024), 1.

16   For more letters, see Dietrich Bonhoeffer, *Letters and Papers from Prison* (Santa Fe: Touchstone, 1997); Marion Denman Frankfurter and Gardner Jackson, eds., *The Letters of Sacco and Vanzetti* (New York: Penguin, 1997); John Howard Lawson and Wesley Robert Wells, *Letters from the Death House* (Los Angeles: Civil Rights Congress, 1953); and Seán Ó Riain and 'Ray,' *Condemned: Letters from Death Row* (Dublin: Liberties, 2008). For collections of personal and critical essays, see *American Prison Writing Archive,* https://prisonwitness.org; Bell Gale Chevigny, ed., *Doing Time: 25 Years of Prison Writing* (New York: Arcade, 2011); David Coogan, ed., *Writing Our Way Out: Memoirs from Jail* (Richmond: Brandylane, 2015); Elsinore Bennu Think Tank, *Life Sentences: Writings from Inside an American Prison* (Cleveland: Belt Publishing, 2019); H. Bruce Franklin, ed., *Prison Writing in 20th-Century America* (New York: Penguin, 1999); Joy James, ed., *The New Abolitionists: (Neo) Slave Narratives and Contemporary Prison Writings* (Albany: State University of New York, 2005); Alice Kim et. al., eds. *The Long Term: Resisting Life Sentences,*

Working Toward Freedom (Chicago: Haymarket Books, 2018); Doran Larson, *Fourth City: Essays from the Prison in America* (East Lansing: Michigan State University Press, 2014); Joe Lockard and Sherry Rankins-Robertson, eds., *Prison Pedagogies: Learning and Teaching with Imprisoned Writers* (Syracuse: Syracuse University Press, 2018); Caits Meissner, ed., *The Sentences That Create Us: Crafting A Writer's Life in Prison* (Chicago: Haymarket Books, 2022); Marie Mulvey-Roberts, ed., *Writing for Their Lives: Death Row U.S.A.* (Urbana: University of Illinois Press, 2007); Ayelet Waldman and Robin Levi, eds., *Inside This Place, Not Of It: Narratives from Women's Prisons* (New York: Verso, 2017).

17   James Baldwin, "An Open Letter to My Sister, Angela Y. Davis," *If They Come in the Morning: Voices of Resistance,* edited by Angela Y. Davis (New York: Verso, 2016).

18   CeCe McDonald, "'Go Beyond Our Natural Selves': The Prison Letters of CeCe McDonald," *Transgender Studies Quarterly* 4, no. 2, ed. Omise'eke Natasha Tinsley (May 2017), 243–65.

19   Prison Letters Project. https://prisonlettersproject.org/; "Prison Letters Responds to Incarcerated People," *Yale Law School Today,* September 19, 2022, https://law.yale.edu/yls-today/news/prison-letters-project-responds -incarcerated-people.

20   Ruth Wilson Gilmore, "Forgotten Places and the Seeds of Grassroots Planning," *Engaging Contradictions: Theory, Politics, and Methods of Activist Scholarship*, ed. Charles R. Hale (Berkeley: University of California Press, 2008), 31–61, http:// www.jstor.org/stable/10.1525/j.ctt1pncnt.7.

21   See Leah Eliot, "The Types of Books We Cannot Send to Prisons (and Why)," *Appalachian Prison Book Project*, April 20, 2023, https:// appalachianprisonbookproject.org/2023/04/20/the-types-of-books-we-cannot -send-to-prisons-and-why/.

22   Jeanie Austin, "Mail Digitization," March 1, 2021, https://jeanieaustin .com/2021/03/01/mail-digitization/; Shruthi Vasudevan, "A State by State Report: Letter Scanning Legislation in Appalachian Prisons and Jails," *Appalachian Prison Book Project*, April 26, 2023, https:// appalachianprisonbookproject.org/2023/04/26/letter-scanning-legislation-in -appalachian-prisons-and-jails/.

23   Marc Falkoff, ed., *Poems from Guantánamo* (Iowa City: University of Iowa Press, 2007).

24   Kaia Stern, "Human Connection is Contraband. So How Do We Do Education?" *Journal of Higher Education in Prison* 1, no.1 (2021): 18–21. Also

see Mariame Kaba and Kelly Hayes, *Let This Radicalize You: Organizing and the Revolution of Reciprocal Care* (Chicago: Haymarket, 2023).

25 See, for instance, Michelle Alexander, *The New Jim Crow: Mass Incarceration in the Age of Colorblindness* (New York: New Press, 2010); Douglass Blackmon, *Slavery By Another Name: The Re-Enslavement of Black Americans from the Civil War to World War II* (New York: Doubleday, 2008); Angela Davis, *Abolition Democracy: Beyond Empire, Prisons, and Torture* (New York: Seven Stories, 2005); Marie Gottschalk, *Caught: The Prison State and the Lockdown of American Politics* (Princeton: Princeton University Press, 2016); Victoria Law, *Resistance Behind Bars: The Struggles of Incarcerated Women* (Oakland: PM Press, 2009); Beth Richie, *Arrested Justice: Black Women, Violence, and America's Prison Nation* (New York: New York University Press, 2012); Bryan Stevenson, *Just Mercy: A Story of Justice and Redemption* (New York: One World, 2015).

26 Maggie Montague, "Books Make Time Move a Little Faster," *Appalachian Prison Book Project*, April 26, 2018, https://appalachianprisonbookproject .org/2018/04/26/books-make-time-move-a-little-faster/.

27 Mariame Kaba, *We Do This 'Til We Free Us: Abolitionist Organizing and Transforming Justice* (Chicago: Haymarket Books, 2021); Angela Y. Davis et al., *Abolition. Feminism. Now.* (Chicago: Haymarket Books, 2022).

28 For a list of prison book projects, see prisonbookprogram.org.

29 We were not able to read this writer's name.

30 West Virginia Center for Budget and Policy, "The High Cost of Mass Incarceration in West Virginia," https://wvpolicy.org/wp-content /uploads/2019/02/WVCBP_IncarcerationInfographic_FINAL.pdf; Kyle Vass, "W.Va. Prisons Data Show Significant Racial Disparity in Recidivist Life Sentencing," *West Virginia Public Broadcasting,* March 22, 2021.

31 Judah Schept, *Coal, Cages, and Crisis: The Rise of the Prison Economy in Central Appalachia* (New York: New York University Press, 2022), 9–13.

32 *Black By God: The West Virginian,* https://blackbygod.org/.

33 See Angela Y. Davis et al., *Abolition. Feminism. Now.* (Chicago: Haymarket Books, 2022); Beth E. Richie, *Arrested Justice: Black Women, Violence, and America's Prison Nation* (New York: New York University Press, 2012); Hugh Ryan, *The Women's House of Detention: A Queer History of a Forgotten Prison* (New York: Bold Type Books, 2022); Eric A. Stanley and Nat Smith, eds., *Captive Genders: Trans Embodiment and the Prison Industrial Complex* (Oakland: AK Press, 2011).

34   Leah Wang, "Prisons are a Daily Environmental Injustice," *Prison Policy Initiative,* April 20, 2022, https://www.prisonpolicy.org/blog/2022/04/20 /environmental_injustice/?mibextid=Zxz2cZ. Also see, Elizabeth Bradshaw, "Tombstone Towns and Toxic Prisons: Prison Ecology and the Necessity of an Anti-Prison Environmental Movement," *Critical Criminology* 26 (2018): 407–22.

35   Judah Schept, *Coal, Cages, and Crisis: The Rise of the Prison Economy in Central Appalachia* (New York: New York University Press, 2022); Brett Story, *Prison Land: Mapping Carceral Power across Neoliberal America* (Minneapolis: University of Minnesota Press, 2019), 79–104.

36   Dwayne Betts, "Could an Ex-Con Become an Attorney? I Intended to Find out," *New York Times Magazine,* October 16, 2018, https://www.nytimes .com/2018/10/16/magazine/felon-attorney-crime-yale-law.html.

37   Danielle Sered, *Until We Reckon: Violence, Mass Incarceration, and the Road to Repair* (New York: New Press, 2019), 34.

38   My gratitude to Nina Johnson for this phrase and for pointing me to the second phrase in adrienne maree brown's *Emergent Strategy: Shaping Change, Changing Worlds* (Chico: AK Press, 2017), 27.

39   Lucille Clifton, *Good Woman: Poems and A Memoir, 1969-1980* (Amherst: University of Massachusetts Press, 1987), 275.

40   Gwendolyn Brooks, *Blacks* (Chicago: Third World Press, 1987), 496.

41   Caleb Smith, ed., introduction to *The Life and the Adventures of a Haunted Convict,* by Austin Reed (New York: Modern Library, 2017), lxvi.

EDITORIAL STATEMENT

*L*ike so much of APBP's work, making this book has been a collective process. The contributions of many people breathe life into our organization. The one principle that united our work and guided many editorial decisions is the commitment to giving letter writers and artists the full respect they deserve. At best, their individual letters offer us small glimpses into their lives, and gathered together, they give us perhaps an even broader understanding of how a human navigates life in a prison or jail in the United States.

We offer here a brief discussion of our editing process, some of the most important editorial challenges, and how we worked through them. These include considerations about how to select and organize material, how to reflect the diversity of the people who write to APBP, how to obtain permissions from contributors, how much editorial commentary to add, and how to incorporate artwork.

In January 2018, a group of APBP volunteers spent hours going through the many letters we've received in the years since we

Dungeon's and Dragons game books New York Crime family criminal Justice
Non Fiction Mafia, James Patterson child psychology CONStellations self help book
ollege Dictionary dictionary A DICTIONARY SIGN LANGUAGE
Thriller or Suspense Nelson's Illustrated Bible Dictionary Dictionary
physics Dictionary, Becoming the Iceman, Science Fiction, Emily Dickerson
9th-20th century comparative literature Spanish vocabulary learning book, bible
istory, History of the Choctaw Indian Tribe (Karl Marx's - communist Manifesto
ing James Bible Vine's Expository Dictionary India Religion. Hindu-"
Crime/Legal Thrillers, Biographies/Auto Biographies
lictionary Please do send me the starting a business/
Business Planning book mentioned in your note English/German Dictionary
otography Books Ductionary NFL Football Rules Almanac Thermodynamic
Dean Koontz DAVID BALDACCI Dictionary Frankenstein
all-Spanish dictionary HighSchool Arithmatic or Pre Algebra Romance sudok
Thesaurus. Dracula construction. Teri wood The Heart Is A Lonely Hunter Non-fiction U.S. Histor
Steve Blakely. plumbing. Kashamba williams
antom Physics. Spirituality. Sister Souljan mythology HUMAN ANATOM
POLITICAL BOOKS Michael baisden Wahida Clark meteorology Dictionary

Patchwork of requests
by Alexus Eudall

began—around 200 per week over almost two decades. Boxes and boxes with thousands of letters. A daunting task. How to choose? We undertook selecting and organizing the rich and varied material in a way that best offers people who read this book a wide perspective and hopefully a deeper understanding of people in confinement and the culture that confines them.

We began curating the letters and artwork by developing a tentative set of common themes based on the observations of long-time volunteers. Using these themes, the volunteers pulled out letters that either spoke to an identified theme or powerfully suggested a new one. Many letters we receive simply state the writer's requests, and we also pulled a number of these to show the wide array of interests displayed. We also looked for letters that gave us insight into the person whose writing we held in our hands—letters that told us about their lives before or during their imprisonment, their hopes for life after their release, their intellectual and political interests, their fears and simple pleasures, their families; their thoughts on the whole kaleidoscope of life. Some of the letters went beyond words, offering us astounding artwork in pencil, pen, or colored markers. These, too, were chosen for the book.

We aimed to find letters that reflect the diversity of people inside prison. America's criminal punishment system disproportionately targets Black people, people of color, poor people, people with disabilities, and other marginalized groups. We searched through our archives, looking for writers from the LGBTQ+ community, Spanish-speaking writers, older and younger writers, writers with disabilities, writers who are veterans, writers from each of the six states to which we send books, writers who practice different religions, and writers of varied ethnicities and racial identities. However, because we only require minimal identifying information to send a book, we do not always know the backgrounds and identities of writers and artists unless they share something about themselves in their letter—sometimes this is a lot of information and sometimes very little. Also, while we try to save every letter, some have been lost, or the writing fades over time and crucial perspectives are left out. Another challenge is knowing that people in prison must censor themselves at times. For fear of retaliation, people in prison may not write as freely about their experiences or conditions as they'd want. In addition, the process of letter writing inherently excludes people who do not know how to write or who do not feel comfortable writing. In other words, letters reveal a great deal, but there is always more to understand.

Once we had a set of potential letters, we created a system to seek permission from all the writers and artists whose work we hoped to include. We wanted them to have the agency and control over their work that they deserve but are so often denied. We sent a letter explaining the book project; expressing our hope to publish their artwork or letters, in full or in part; and inviting them to fill out a permission form if they were interested in contributing. The form offered them the opportunity to specify with what name they wanted us to identify their work. The letter also invited them to write an additional essay about how access to books has impacted them.

Getting permission from contributors proved complicated. People can be transferred, and their mail is not forwarded. Return addresses are sometimes outdated, incomplete, or hard to read. After waiting a few months for a response, we sent another round of letters to those we had not heard from, using the online locators each state provides to update addresses when possible. Sometimes we discovered a writer or artist had been transferred or released with no forwarding address. In a few cases, the person had died. Meanwhile new letters kept coming in, and many were good candidates for the book, so new permission requests were sent. We sent contributors updates on the progress of this book as we worked toward publication.

In our early years, quotations from letters were often shared among volunteers without accompanying names. We opted to include a few of these even though we have little to no identifying information and were unable to locate the writer. In these instances, we used only states or otherwise marked these contributions as unknown to try to honor both the person's work and privacy. We plan to create a website with additional materials and will invite individuals to reach out if they recognize their words and want to be identified. We welcome suggestions about these editorial practices.

In the end, we were able to secure permissions for the vast majority of letters and all of the artwork included in the book. Once permission was granted, volunteers scanned and typed letters without any editorial changes to spelling, grammar, or punctuation. Then we arranged the writing into categories or themes. While we included some letters in full, we mainly used excerpts of letters to highlight common issues. We added a chapter that focuses on the book clubs and higher education classes that APBP has supported inside prisons.

Each chapter begins with a short preface. We remain painfully aware how easy it is to impose our own narratives on this primary material and create a distorted view. Beyond a name and the content of their letters, we do not presume to know the people who write to us. We tried to keep the editorial voice at a minimum to avoid forcing our own narratives and assumptions onto the writers and artists within the book. It was always our intention to make editorial changes sparingly and respectfully.

Sometimes we made difficult decisions that detract from the original feel and sensibility of the letters. For example, we decided to use typed versions of the letters rather than scans of handwritten ones to allow the reader to better focus on the content of each letter. Also, many writers refer to themselves and others as "inmates" or "prisoners." We at times let this language stand and at other times shifted to people-centered language. A certain accumulative force was emerging with the repetition of labels that many find offensive.[1] And we knew we were responsible for that. APBP has always advocated for person-first language; we also recognize that language usage continues to be an important debate and a matter of personal preference among incarcerated people, community activists, and scholars.

Similarly, we made minor copy edits to letters and quotes for clarity and flow while keeping the writing true to what each person wrote as it distinguishes their individuality and creative flourish. We opted to retain underlining when used for emphasis by letter writers but input italics for book titles for clarity and consistency. We removed references to specific prisons, jails, or information that might expose letter-writers to retaliation or harm. Ellipses indicate when a small portion of the letter was omitted.

From its earliest conception, this book featured not only letters but artwork. Some letters impressed the volunteers well before they were opened, as the envelopes came decked out in some truly inspiring artwork. With so many pieces, it was difficult to choose artwork for the book. In an ideal world, we would gladly include all of it. But we had to rein in our enthusiasm and accede to legal and financial constraints. We had to rule out any copyrighted images, however well-wrought Mickey and Tigger might be. And we had to consider the high costs of printing images in color.

Through this book, we hope to create space for incarcerated writers and artists to be seen, to bring attention to the conditions they face that perpetuate harm, and to demonstrate the power of reading and education inside prisons and jails. The exchange of books, letters, and artwork has proven to be a powerful catalyst for connecting people and building community. We continue to receive letters and artwork that reveal something new to us about the United States prison system, that change our outlook on the world, that inform us of a book we've never heard of, and that show us a small part of the person on the other side.

Notes

1   Eddie Ellis, "An Open Letter to Our Friends on the Question of Language," *Center for NU Leadership on Urban Solutions*, May 21, 2020, https://perma.cc/JQ67-UKHZ; Akiba Solomon, "What Words We Use—and Avoid—When Covering People and Incarceration," *Marshall Project*, April 12, 2021, https://www.themarshallproject.org/2021/04/12/what-words-we-use-and-avoid-when-covering-people-and-incarceration.

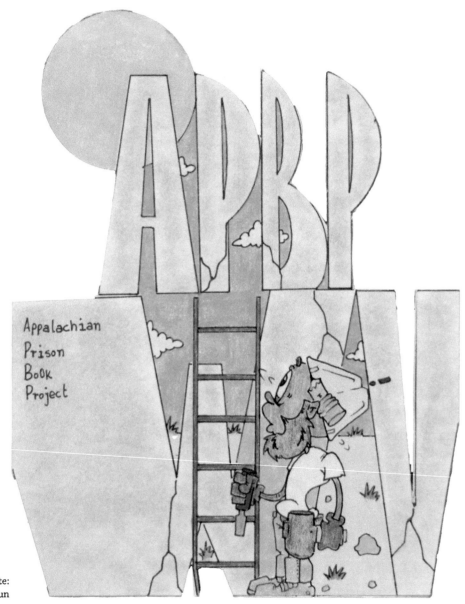

This page and opposite:
Art by O. Ogun

Chapter 1

BOOK REQUESTS

*R*eading can be many things. It can be an escape or a distraction. It can be a means to knowledge acquisition. It can be an act of faith. For those living in punitive carceral settings, reading can be a lifebelt, a realized dream, a way out.

Where there is no physical escape, reading is a door to another world. In her essay "Almost like Freedom," Jane Garner writes about the power of removing oneself physically and emotionally through reading and library spaces. Her research, a collection of accounts from incarcerated individuals, reinforces the need for book access and illustrates how people use books as an "escape from the crowded, noisy conditions in which they live and the aggressive or violent behaviors they sometimes experience in their cellblocks."[1] Reading is not a cure-all, but it is certainly a necessary sanctuary.

Access to books can also enhance people's ability to gather knowledge and pursue emotional growth. Megan Sweeney, author of *Reading Is My Window: Books and the Art of Reading in Women's Prisons*,

Reading is power. Reading is knowledge. Reading is being free.

—Tanner Hartman

notes that incarcerated people use reading "to come to terms with their pasts, to negotiate their present experiences, and to reach toward different futures."[2] In particular, Sweeney studies the effect of popular genres such as narratives of victimization, African American urban fiction, and self-help books, though she notes that she "could write a second book about women's readings of the thrillers, mysteries, true crime books, vampire stories, and contemporary and historical romances."[3] From autobiographies and self-help to vampires and romance, people who are incarcerated read anything and everything that people do on the outside. The only difference, as both Garner and Sweeney note, is incarcerated individuals' lack of access to reading materials, which we discuss further in the next chapter.

As many of the excerpts in this section suggest, books help people avoid the intellectual and spiritual stagnancy carceral settings too often encourage. Some of the most requested books at APBP are dictionaries, language books, thesauri, almanacs, and legal primers. We also receive many requests for a variety of religious texts related to Wicca, Islam, Judaism, Buddhism, and Christianity. Our organization struggles to keep these resources on our shelves.

New volunteers are often perplexed when they notice the number of requests for reference books like dictionaries and almanacs. Approximately one in six books that we mail fall into this category. The reason for this phenomenon is simple yet overlooked. Incarcerated people have limited access to the internet and the constant flow of information that people on the outside so often take for granted. Darrin Lester, a core APBP member who spent many years in prison, explains: "Why do they want an almanac? Because you are always arguing on the yard about something. Even if it is sports, it could be whatever. They will say 'no he did not, he was not drafted,' and then they will say 'I'll go get the almanac,' so now it becomes a settler."[4] The almanac serves as the "prison internet."

More than anything, the requests we receive at APBP reflect the varied interests of those who write to us—we never know what to expect when we open a letter.

Kaleidoscope of Interests

"I have come to the well again, looking to fill my dipper with the knowledge I desire. I am a Two Spirited Native American seeking literature on American Indian Religious practices."

—LoRee Hernandez

"It's hard to believe that there is actually a group like yours pro-viding books to us, especially trying to match our interest with the book you send! Bless you! I just finished reading the Harry Potter series back-to-back! (twice!) and now I'm suffering from 'Post-Potter Depression,' because I wish the series would just go on and on. So, I borrowed book #1 from a fellow criminal and I'm going to start all over again."

—VA

"I was wondering if I could request a book about dreams if that could be possible."

—VA

"I would LOVE to have some more comic books. Marvel or DC. But I like Marvel better. Here are some names of comic books to get. *Batman - The Killing Joke / Harley Quinn - Night and Day / Harley Quinn and Her Gang of Harleys / Marvel Encyclopedia / Wolverine / Avengers & X-Men Axis* ------> And here is some more by Stephen Jones called - *The Mammoth Book of Nightmare Stories*, and *Halloween Stories* -----> PLEASE And thank you for your time and your support at my time of need. Hit me back as soon as you can. Let me know how things are going your way. Stay safe much LOVE"

—Dominic D. Brown

"I love hood an street novels by black authors only! This is what eye relate 2 . . .

Authors I Luv
Carl Weber
Wahida Clark
Nikki Turner
Treasure Hernandez
Sister Souljah
Joy Deja King
K. Elliott
Norie
Omar Tyree
T.I.
Eminem
50
Michael Covington
Dorian Sykes
Brittani Williams
K. Roland Williams
Michael Baisden
Terri Woods
Quentin Carter
Marcus Major
Tameka Scott"

—Anton'Ari Alexander

"My interests are more on the academic side with preference to history, biography, Jewish Studies, 19th–20th century comparative literature, quality current fiction, the sciences (readable by the layman) including cosmology/astronomy, and birds and animals (e.g. *Wesley the Owl* was a delight). Particulars on my wish list, Dickens' *Martin Chuzzlewit*, Thomas Mann's two volume *Joseph* . . . Balzac is always good."

—David

"I am writing in regards to the books that you sent me last week. I wanted to thank you very much. The dictionary will be used a lot and the other book was very good. I managed to read it in only 5 days. It was *The Heart Is a Lonely Hunter* by Carson McCullers. I would like to receive more books as soon as possible."

—Gregory Fitzgerald

"The most compelling book I've read thus far is *Fearless—The Adam Brown Story*. It was truly inspiring. A story of courage, change and commitment to family and God."

—Marc A. Perrelli

"I would like a book on how-to manuals or sports (Memphis Grizzlies) (basketball) and a Christianity book."

—Misty Rifenburg

"My friend wants to know do you have Spanish books? He only reads in Spanish."

—TN

"I am requesting the following books, if available: Book on the Choctaw Indian Tribe with picture references and historic data concerning the tribe. Herbal relief of the body through the use of different plants and berries found in nature. Detailed picture of the plants and berries used and details on their relief capabilities."

—Jerome

"I love fantasy books. I have really wanted to start the Dungeons & Dragons series about Drizzt Do'Urden but our library does not have the first of the series. I am currently reading *The Name of the Wind* by Patrick Rothfuss, it's pretty good. It has a similar voice as *The Outlander*. There is a second by Rothfuss called *The Wise Man's Fear*, if it's possible to receive a copy of that, that would be great. I am an avid graphic novel/manga fan. Any would do. I am also studying music theory. I have played guitar for close to 25 years now, figured now is as good a time as any to try and understand what it is that I am doing :) Is there a dictionary specifically devoted to musical terms? I would love something like that. I practice Buddhism. I would love a collection of Sutras, or literature that deeply explains Samsara. I love poetry. My favorite poet being Sylvia Plath. . . . . Finally, I am part of the prison college program so a collegiate dictionary would be greatly appreciated."

—WV

"Buenos días me gustaría si por favor me podrían mandar un libro para aprender 'Crochet Stitch' en español por favor. Muchas gracias. Que dios los vendiga."

—OH

"Thank you for my last book *The Backyard Homestead*. It will help me on the outside. In the back it shows other Backyard Books like *The Backyard Homestead Seasonal Planner*, *The Backyard Homestead Book of Building Projects* (may like the most), *The Backyard Homestead Guide to Raising Farm Animals*, and *The Backyard Homestead Kitchen Know-How*. I'm into woodworking, Blacksmithing, off-grid living, solar power, love to use upcycled projects, I like to use my hands to make neat stuff. If you all are out of this kind of book I'd like a ghost stories book."

—David

"I seem to recall the first book, other than Golden Books, I consumed was *Boxcar Children*. The next book that has impacted me more than any other is entitled *In Search of the Miraculous* by P.D. Ouspensky. Even before I was brought to prison as a relatively young man I read a great deal, however, once I entered secure-confinement I became a voracious consumer of the written word."

—Jake

"Please send me any books you have on dogs. I'm an avid dog lover. I have 3 dogs at home. Also if you have any books on the state of Montana, please send me those."

—TN

"My fiancee is Latino (Panamanian). Asking for Spanish vocab. Trying to get one for awhile. I want to also recite my vows in Spanish."

—TN

"I pray for you all and the world every night. God bless us all. I am writing you about a few books on black history like Huey Newton a Black Panther Activist and Marcus Garvey a Black Activist. I would love the both of them to have and read."

—Dewey

"I'm from East TN the Mountains and for us like for many other Appalachians church is a way of life. Will you please please please send me any books wrote on SNAKE handling."

—TN

"*1984* exceeds my request and I would probably say is much more exciting, and revolutionary. Thank you for this new edition to my literary library."

—Horace Nunley

"I have a few requests. And I was hoping you could help me out with some. So here's a list, and thank you so much!

1. A composition book
2. A sketch pad (to draw)
3. A 2023 calendar (with pictures please)
4. Anything to do with antiques/collectables
5. Anything to do with stones and their energies and/or wicca/witchcraft
6. Haunted places (with pictures)
7. A book with beautiful pictures."

—TN

"Thank you for the recent gift (*Sense and Sensibility* by Jane Austen). I've enjoyed all of the Austen novels I've read. In fact, I've enjoyed all the classical literature you have sent me, including *Emma*!"

—OH

"I am especially interested in technical materials. I am keen on the study of meteorology [atmospheric phenomenons] and any related materials to said subject. My ongoing passion includes: various modes of communications—Amateur radio by way of voice and International Morse Code [. . . (my previous radio call signs < when I lived in Chicago, Illinois, and Seattle, Washington–respectively >)]."[5]

—Clara Bess

"Thank you for helping us in these circumstances.

- Histories of baseball prior to 1950 (Ruth, Gehrig, Rizzuto)
- People who rode passenger trains and street cars pre 1950 including sports teams; the western bound Orphan Train, etc.
- Memoirs of NY Street Arabs— Golden, Canter, Greeley, Sarnoff, Covello, Lefcourt, etc.
- Bios of candymen (Hershey, Mars, etc.), stores (Field, Stewart, Woolworth, Wanamaker, etc.), railroad magnates, restaurants (Johnson, etc.), fast-food (Kroc, Thomas, etc.) and food (Heinz)
- Non-fiction U.S. History—growth of cities, inventions, construction
- History Press, Arcadia, historical photos (USA)

We get out 4½ hours a week so I can give books to others."

—Bob

"Thanks again for sending a book recently. *The Hood* looks very interesting and already has a list of guys that want to read it when I finish. . . . Please do send me the starting a business/business planning book mentioned in your note if still available! Exactly what I need!"

—Warren Anderson

"I have always been fascinated with the sky—not only weather patterns (which I do love!) but anything dealing with it—weather, sun, moon, stars, storms, constellations, planets—all of it absolutely fascinates me. If we could find a book on the sky for me, I would love it very much."

—TN

"I would like to thank you and the APBP for the book I received, it's good to read in my native Russian language."

—Mykhaylo Botsyvnyuk

"Here are some topics of interest: Effective Communication, Healthy Relationships, Conflict Resolution, Parenting, Values, Fatherless Homes, Adolescent Culture, Social Action, Domestic Violence, Leadership, and anything you may deem worthy."

—Gordon Atkeison

"As always I have a long and very varied list of books here: *Out of Africa* by Isak Dinesen, (I hope this is correct) *Forest Magic* by Robin Hobb, *Noblehouse, Shogun* (I know, how many times I've lost that book?) *The Children's Story* all by James Clavell, *Paper and Fire* by Rachel Caine, *61 Hours, Nothing to Lose* or *Nothing but Trouble* (can't remember which) by Lee Child. *Nova War* by Gary Gibson, *The Emperor's Blades* by Steve Blakely, or any other book you choose. As always whatever you bless me with will be greatly appreciated and read then passed around and read some more again + again. I really can't explain the joy you guys bring us hopeless convicts. They say the man that reads lives a thousand lives. I agree. I have been locked up nine years day for day come October 30. Here in TN, but I've spent nights (and days) in Westeros and Slaver's Bay, in New York City, in Feudal Japan alongside Toranaga and the Anjin-San, on the moons of planets in galaxies with names I can't pronounce and apparently can't spell. So thanks again. Even just writing to you guys makes this ole Mingo County boy's heart beat a little stronger. Life is what you give. You put life in an envelope or box, put a stamp on it and mail it out. Thanks for giving life. P.S. Go Mountaineers!"

—Ashley Van Natter

Learning and Expanding Horizons

"I am frequently asked how I have been able to tolerate decades of oppressive enslavement. Invariably, my response is that I refuse to put my mind in a cage and I read a great deal. APBP plays a starring role for many of us who are expanding our horizons by reading."

　　—Jake

"I greatly appreciate the Italian Books some 5–6 months ago. My Italian isn't perfetto (perfect) it's more medio (average). I don't claim to be a scholar but I know a lot more than when I started learning it. And for that I feel molta benedetto (very blessed). The feeling I get from receiving anything from someone/anyone I've never met personally before is amazingly warm and fulfilling. Molto sinceramente (Very sincerely)!!"

　　—Steven

"So far the books you have sent have been very helpful: the one helped me obtain my GED! The car book will also help me a lot on my 68 Plymouth road runner that's been covered up in my garage for a very long time!"

　　—KY

"Here is what I would like for your Project to try and help me with. I would like to have a good Dictionary. English. And a good Law Book on legal Issues. And a copy of *Prisoner's Rights*. And you know Basic Law's felonies and misdemeanors. I know a little about some laws. But I would love to have some law Books so I could look at them. And maybe help out others."

—Steve Rauhuff

"Dear Brethren! I'm in need of dictionary– used or new if you can please send it to me. I'm not doing good with money–so I can't pay you. God bless you!"

—Polo

"*As a Man Thinketh* by James Allen. This book transformed me. It taught me that if we want to live a beautiful life we must think beautiful thoughts. It encouraged me to stay centered in the highest principles of love, truth, justice, benevolence, acceptance and responsibility, among other spiritual ideals."

—Mark Sims

"Thanks for *The Handy Science Answer Book*. I'm gonna take many journeys in it. *Mark Twain's Complete Short Stories* I have taken many hours of adventures through his writing and he's a character and has good humor. It's helping me be more open minded to how I write and the way I write. I feel like you are heaven sent. Thanks and I want to ask you to keep an eye out for a dictionary. I need one bad. Mine is a hand me down and has pages missing and it is in 3 pieces but I still am holding on to it. Thanks again, and the last 3 selections have been my kinda reading."

—Toby R. Lambert

"I have been incarcerated for 4 years and 4 months now and have learned to read and write in that time."

—TN

"I would like to use this time to read up, learn, and take the time learning about my heritage which is Native American. I'm actually Seneca Indian (Seneca Nation of Indians) and the tribe is out of New York, Salamanca, Irving, as well as other counties from that state. When I was younger my gramma tried to sit down with me and teach me the language and whatnot about our tribe and of course I ain't interested. Well now that I'm older and have the time as well with wanting to know and learn more about my nationality and tribe. If your department can help me out with my request it would be highly appreciated plus a wonderful blessing."

—Daniel

"Over the years I never was good at math. I wrote APBP and they sent me a workbook on Algebra. I wrote them requesting something on the Japanese language and received a book on that. Later I got a Spanish dictionary. Can you imagine an inmate coming home speaking 2 foreign languages? Out in the world time goes by fast. You never really have time for anything. In prison time goes by slowly and you have nothing but time on your hands. Why not use that time wisely and pick up on a book and learn something?"

—Miles T.

"Thank you for all you have done for me in 2013 in my college education. All semesters I made the Dean's list. I'm also doing good with my Spanish."

—OH

"I am currently in the dog program, we train dogs that come from the humane society and try to get them adopted, as a trainer I strive to be better at what I do, so I am requesting if you could send me some books on how to train dogs and how to become a better dog trainer. I appreciate your time and effort if you could locate and send me some books."

—David Willett

"A few months ago I received 2 books and I was amazed to find out that your organization truly existed and gave out free books! Your organization has made it a bit easier for me because I'm big on education, knowledge, and wisdom. I currently have a huge chunk of time, but I count this as a blessing because I can use this time to catch up on my studies. I actually want to be a mathematician, a scientist, and a scholar. I know it's pretty much impossible to know everything, but I can't help but want to know everything. By the time I get released I'm hoping I can tackle at least 2 of my goals. I truly appreciate your assistance in receiving books, and I hope I can continue getting books from your services."

—C. S. Mars

"Your work reforms and helps those that can't understand how to reintegrate back into society. Thanks to many of your books we're able to learn new skills, or better prepare ourselves for what life has in store for us once we're back. Many can't find jobs, or choose to return to their old habits, but some of the books we obtain from y'all help to confront the mistakes that led us here. Through reading we can place ourselves in certain situations that can be reformed with better choices. A recent book I obtained from you months ago on the current Syrian conflict, helped me reevaluate my own life, as things could be worse as the circumstances of my life could mimic more of the current armed struggle.

Every day could be much worse, but I go into life knowing things can change for the better with an optimistic mindset. I educate myself with the political and historical books you send me. The more I learn, the less likely I'll be willing to turn to crime to make a living, due to my ignorance of the many opportunities still open to me. The books I obtain are wonderful and I'd be grateful for more political and historical books, to expand my knowledge and reform my ways. Knowledge will free me, and help me to never return to a cell."

—Horace Nunley

"Thank you for the Do It Yourself Reader's Digest book you sent me. That helped me refresh my knowledge on electric, plumbing and other stuff. I just started to work maintenance here."

—TN

"Thank you for sending a dictionary to me. It helped me write a letter back home."

—TN

"The importance of reading can instruct us to accomplish certain goals in our lives such as learning a trade or putting a toy together for your child or children. Reading can also stimulate our brains so that we can think more clearly and make better decisions for ourselves and others such as our kids."

—David Willett

"Reading and studying seems to be one of the very few ways of helping me not to make this a complete waste of time, and when I learn something it also gives me a feeling of accomplishment."

—Jason Collins

"Could you locate a book based on the multiple ideologies that were a part of the Black Liberation Movement. Specifically Black power era. Also, a dictionary."

—Eric R. Thomas

"I really thank you for the legal primer and *The Complete Law School Companion*. I really loved Ellen Greenberg's *Supreme Court Explained* and it's gonna come in real handy cause I [am helping] 2 men in the Court of Appeals Fourth District. Something tells me I'm gonna have to file writs of certiorari to the U.S. Supreme Court."

—WV

"You are educating and blessing us with a wonderful gift and treasure called 'a book.' You give us the importance of life which is love. A book helps us free our minds from prison and through some of these books we also find God or a better path in life. I have enjoyed each book that I have received. I've read books on history, religion, and art, others on trades and how to start up a non-profit organization using a 501c3 manuscript. Your help and blessings are preparing me for a better life and future after incarceration. Reading books has inspired me to write a poetry book. Thank you for the beautiful work you have created my friends."

—Dewey

"Speaking of such things, you wouldn't think a thing like a G.E.D. dictionary would make all that much difference, but it helped me brush up on some things I had forgotten, and it helped a youngster who was convinced he couldn't learn and was on the verge of quitting school to go on and pass his pretest. I lost track of him after that. He was either moved to the other side of this place, or transferred to another institution, but I'm sure he went on to get his G.E.D. He was just too proud and fired up after passing his pretest not to have went on to get his G.E.D. He told me he missed out on some good jobs because of not being able to fill out the job application, so it'll make a big difference in his life when he gets out."

—Robin Mayes

Healing Sanctuaries

"I was locked up at the age of 17 and I've not been free since then. I'm 33 now. After 16 years, almost everyone I knew is faded away. Yet, I look forward to getting mail from you and seeing what type of adventure you will take me on next. Sometimes this cell can seem like a tomb and a book is a way to leave, if only for a day or two."

—Hugh Williams, Jr.

"Hello, my name is Tanner, and if you're some of the few reading this, we might have some things in common. One, being incarcerated. The second being a thirst for good books. Whether it's horror, fantasy, mystery, or nonfiction, reading can be a very useful way of letting your mind escape within these walls. It also helps you keep your mind sharper, which is important being in jail or prison, which is why I want to thank my sister and her friends at the Appalachian Prison Book Project for all their work helping prisoners in the system to be able to get books more easily. Reading is power. Reading is knowledge. Reading is being free."

—Tanner Hartman

"I have M.S. and am bound to a wheelchair so I spend most of my time reading. I don't have anyone on the outside that can help me with finances or packages. You are very special people to do this for us. Reading takes my mind off of my situation. It transports me to different lands, tests my ability to solve murder/mystery, and laugh at the comedy."

—Joseph Morgan

"Thank you so much for the dictionary and Bible. I especially like the Bible. It is the most explanatory Bible I've ever had . . . I probably already told you but my 91-year-old grandma is taking care of my mother, her daughter is 72 and they have had strokes last year. My mother had one the worst. She had one one day and my grandma had one the next day. My mother has diabetes, dementia, and psychosis. I really need to learn all I can so I can be of more help to my grandmother and mother. My grandmother has dementia too."

—VA

"Being that I do not have a TV, books are how I pass my time. I love reading because when I am in the story, I am not where I really am! :) Thank you for your time and for what you do for us that do not have money for TVs and such."

—TN

"The power of a Good Book can open one's eyes and mind. Can take you out of the place you are In. And put you in a Better place."

—David

"I'm kinda going through some personal issues as far as sobriety. I need some help. I seen there was self help books as a category. So Addiction."

—TN

"When I started writing this, I intended to write a few lines asking for another book on health and wellness, but I got carried away once I thanked you for the book on meditation. You do way more good than you know and deserve to be told so. Thanks to you all for being who you are and for doing what you do. Stay safe until the coronavirus is being talked about as a thing of the past, and whatever you do, don't listen to a thing Trump says."

—Bob C.

"I am currently struggling with the stress of prison and health issues that are being ignored and a couple books would be great medicine."

—TN

"Shhh . . . listen. You can hear some pages flippin,' over the whisperin' . . . NOT!! This prison is a mad house. It's pandemonium. Lunatics and 'crash outs' - Explodin' with no one to take the trash out. All these short timers . . . it appears I'll be the last out. But I've got 'class' now. And not the kind ya gotta sit through . . . Well, I took a few of those, but I meant the kind of class ya get when ya grow. The kind ya get from playin' chess. The kind ya get when ya show some respect. Especially when everything is especially difficult . . . Ya just lost yer truck, dog, and yer shirt. You lost two uncles and a grandma . . . Ya wanna go berzerk and grab some jerk . . . But you don't. Instead you play some handball . . . Put on a brave face . . .

Go shower and shave. Wait in line for a day to make a pre-paid phone call. Pray that someone answers. Feel like an asshole, and hang up–without speakin' a word. Contemplate burnin' some herb . . . Then, make it a verb. Turn on some tunes and ya tune out . . . Damn . . . I think they called 'count.' I'm gettin' around to the point of this paper . . . To thankin' these ladies for six years of favors . . . A big book of birds and a lapidary dictionary, handyman handouts and puzzle books, like pictionary. You are visionaries—in the sense that you noticed a need. You've helped thousands of us . . . without an ounce of greed. You shone through like sunshine and enhanced our minds. And even when it took a while . . . those books showed up right on time."

—Alex-The-Wulff

Envelope Art by Alex-The-Wulff

"All books are truly appreciated. I really think that what you are doing is a wonderful thing. Books help a lot when in jail. It is a true release of stress in much needed times."

—Gregory Fitzgerald

"Today the mailman said my name and I walked up to him happy. There on his cart was a good ole Western to send me out of this jail and into the wild west."

—VA

"I was diagnosed with cancer 3½ years ago, colon cancer. It's in remission now, praise god. I'm looking for some health and books on diet, what not to do for colon cancer problems. There are not very much of med help books here."

—TN

"When the door's locked; the guards have fed you, and all your freedom and dignity has been stripped the only thing left is your mind, the only thing they can never take from you. . . . When all is lost you find salvation in a book."

—Horace Nunley

"I have had a hard time but I am beginning to get my verve again. I just keep meditating and working out and writing and trying to be cool to the people that annoy me and keep in mind that I am annoying too sometimes . . . I have been doing a new meditation that includes me sitting and thanking my higher self for every beautiful perfectly working part of my body and every beautifully designed element of the big world we live in—the magnificence of the bees and the placement of the starsss . . . I find so little space for judgment and negativity when this fills my space. This is the source of creativity. I know I am preaching to the choir, right?"

—Celeste Monet Blair

Notes

1. Jane Garner, "'Almost like Freedom': Prison Libraries and Reading as Facilitators of Escape," *The Library Quarterly* 90, no. 1 (2020): 11, https://doi.org/10.1086/706309.
2. Megan Sweeney, *Reading Is My Window: Books and the Art of Reading in Women's Prisons* (Chapel Hill: University of North Carolina Press, 2010), 1.
3. Sweeney, *Reading Is My Window*, 67.
4. McKenna Galloway, "It's More than Just a Book: How the Appalachian Prison Book Project Is Changing Lives One Page at a Time," *Times West Virginian*, June 10, 2023, https://www.timeswv.com/news/life/it-s-more-than-just-a-book-how-the-appalachian-prison-book-project-is-changing/article_db7c5550-061b-11ee-ba98-1b9a64e8cc44.html.
5. Omitted radio call signs.

Chapter 2
ACCESS AND RESTRICTIONS

It's a sad day when one cannot receive books in prison. I feel like I'm in a Ray Bradbury novel.

—VA

Today the carceral system is more opaque and isolating than ever. This is by design. In the colonial period, prisons were used to detain people until they could be punished, often as a public spectacle.[1] As part of major reform efforts after the American Revolution, modern penitentiaries emerged and "incarceration became the punishment itself."[2] Extreme isolation and labor were branded as rehabilitation methods. After the Civil War, the criminal legal system and convict leasing became a means to re-enslave newly freed people and to extract profit again from coerced unpaid labor.[3]

Prisons and jails are meant to erase people. The public cannot easily see inside these closed institutions. Julian Hawthorne writes in his 1914 prison narrative: "Let every judge, attorney general, district attorney, and jurymen at a trial spend a bona fide term in jail, and there would be no more convictions–prisons would end. Every convict and ex-convict knows that, and eternity will be too short to obliterate that knowledge in him."[4] Visitors, family members, friends, lawyers, and educators must go through background checks, a strict dress code, metal detectors, questioning, monitored visits, and often travel long distances. It's nearly impossible for those not impacted to comprehend what it's like to spend any amount of time in a prison or jail. As Mariame Kaba notes, "isolation itself is actually brutal."[5]

Prison conditions and restrictions came into more public focus during the uprising in Attica in 1971. As recounted by Heather Ann Thompson in *Blood in the Water: The Attica Uprising of 1971 and Its Legacy* and Orisanmi Burton in *Tip of the Spear: Black Radicalism, Prison Repression, and the Long Attica Revolt*, people inside Attica took control of the prison to demand better conditions, such as religious freedom, medical treatment, higher paying jobs, an end to physical abuse, access to toothbrushes and showers and to books and newspapers.[6] Reporters were invited inside Attica to document negotiations between the imprisoned people and the prison administrators. The amount of media attention was unprecedented. The uprising ultimately ended in tragedy with forty-three people dead, almost all of whom were killed by police, correctional officers, and other members of the state when they regained control of the prison.

The issues prompted by the uprising at Attica persist today. Basic access to healthcare, safety, and sanitary living conditions is not ensured. People inside have limited ability to advocate for themselves. On top of this, the right to read a book, whether to learn a skill or expand one's imagination, is often met with suspicion and a myriad of restrictions. The United States spends more than 80 billion

Envelope Art by Todd
Maddox

dollars a year to keep people behind bars, but little of this spending is directed toward books and educational programs.[7] Many libraries are not well-maintained or restocked and can be difficult to access because of limited hours and a set number of people allowed inside at a time. Some people who write to us indicate that they see book carts more than library spaces. Book access and title selection are sparse.

Lack of funding and space are not the only reasons libraries in prisons are neglected. The debate about whether people inside are worthy of reading is always in question. People in power—all the way up to the Supreme Court—have shaped access to books in prison libraries. The 1977 decision in *Bounds v. Smith* made it so state prisons must provide access to people trained in law or a law library. But as Kathrina Sarah Litchfield points out, "Although this did mean that prisoners' access to legal information was legitimized, the rest of the prison library was neglected, both financially and dogmatically."[8] In

Reading Is My Window, Megan Sweeney writes extensively about the 2006 *Beard v. Banks* decision that denied people in a Pennsylvania prison the right to secular newspapers and magazines. She writes that the majority opinion "constructs reading as a privilege that best serves the penal system when it is denied to uncooperative prisoners."[9]

Many organizations have formed to address the need for reading materials. Prison book projects date to the early 1970s, and now more than fifty organizations across the country send free books to people in prisons. In "Prisoners' Right to Read: An Interpretation of the Library Bill of Rights," the American Library Association argues that there is "a compelling public interest in the preservation of intellectual freedom" for those in U.S. prisons.[10] Jeanie Austin and colleagues contend that prison book projects are the organizations that are actually "shouldering the burden of providing information and combatting censorship within prisons, which should, ostensibly, fall within the purview of LIS [Library and Information Science]."[11] R. Dwayne Betts founded Freedom Reads, an organization that makes books more accessible and advocates for beauty in carceral settings. Freedom Reads designs special bookshelves to be placed in housing units or prison libraries: a quiet place to select a book, read, think, and study.

Health books have been returned to APBP because they contain drawings of the human body. Art books rejected because they contain pictures of famous nude sculptures. Someone wrote to us that they were denied romance novels with gay characters. The reason given by the prison on the "Rejected Publication" form said: "[t]he book contains sexually explicit material. This information is determined to be detrimental to the security and good order of the institution and could facilitate criminal activity." In its 2019 "Literature Locked Up" report, PEN America provided the following examples: a federal prison in Colorado refused Barack Obama's memoirs because they were "potentially detrimental to national security," a decision that was eventually reversed.[12] A New York prison attempted to ban a book of maps of the moon because it would "present risks of escape"; a Tennessee prison rejected a book about the Holocaust because it contained photographs of naked victims; Texas prisons have censored *The Color Purple* and books on the civil rights movement.[13] In a historical overview of book restrictions, Sweeney also mentions books that critique racism. The ACLU National Prison Project continues to challenge unreasonable bans.[14]

In the name of security and order, there is little room for reading materials that critique the prison system or contextualize people's lives inside larger structures. Carileigh Jones writes, "Because maintaining control is of paramount importance to prison officials, they hold that objective over and above anything else, including education, and deny anything that they feel might place it in jeopardy. Juxtaposed to this, however, is the fact that incarcerated and formerly incarcerated individuals consistently point to the fact that critical material is what changed and broadened their perspectives."[15] In an essay in the *New York Times*, Christopher Blackwell addresses this contradiction as he describes his experience with book bans in prison:

> Claiming such bans are necessary for the safety and security of prisons seems ludicrous. If anything, many banned books could con-

tribute to a safer environment in prisons and in the societies incarcerated individuals are released into. Practically every author I have encountered while in prison, from Don Miguel Ruiz to Angela Y. Davis, has played a role in my efforts to grow and become a better person—someone who can live in society by adding to it, as opposed to taking from it.[16]

We come across similar statements routinely in letters to APBP.

The main obstacle to sending reading materials is policies that require books be mailed directly from a distributor or publisher. We have a list of about thirty prisons and jails in our region with this policy. PEN America calls these content-neutral restrictions the largest book ban in the country.[17] These restrictions effectively prevent people from reading, as they cannot afford to pay for books, and neither can their families or friends. Many times, we have learned that a prison or jail we have been sending to for years is no longer accepting our books. When this happens, we try to contact that prison or jail, explain our processes, and ask for permission to send books again.

Officials say that the mailing of books must be restricted to curtail contraband, especially drugs. Drug and alcohol-related deaths in state prisons rose 611% between 2001 and 2018.[18] It is a crisis within a crisis. There are effective ways to address the drivers of addiction. Going after books is not one of them. An investigation by the *Texas Tribune* and the Marshall Project found that as many drugs ended up in Texas prisons during the pandemic, when mail was slowed and visits suspended, as in years past.[19] John Lennon, a journalist imprisoned in New York, addresses the harm of prohibiting used books and explains what would improve outcomes for people: "Restrictive policies didn't deter me from smuggling drugs. Opportunity did."[20]

One person sent us a copy of an "inmate request form" they submitted to the prison after one of the books we sent to him was rejected. On the form, he asked why the book was rejected, and the response from the prison reads: "Items utilizing third parties have a higher chance of contraband entering the facility." In a follow-up request to the prison, the person asked whether any contraband had ever entered the prison through books sent from organizations like ours. The response from the prison reads: "Further conversation into the safety and security of this facility will not be discussed."

We occasionally hear directly from a prison or jail that wants to *increase* access to books, and we are happy to hammer out new procedures together.

Prison-distributed tablets are offered by many corrections departments as the solution to contraband; these devices offer secure communication options and access to entertainment and sometimes education. Tablets should be widely available in prisons and jails at no cost to confined people, especially since people in prison are not able to make a living wage. Any work offered to imprisoned people typically pays less than a dollar per hour, often much less. Some people who write to us can hardly afford the stamps to send a letter requesting a free book. More often, however, tablets are unfairly priced; they can break without refund and be withheld by authorities; purchased materials can be lost; and availability can be restricted to certain times or populations.

Corporations offering tablets are primed to take advantage of the high demand and restricted access to books inside prisons. In 2019, Global Tel Link (GTL), now ViaPath Technologies, contracted with the West Virginia Divisions of Corrections and Rehabilitation to offer "free" tablets to people inside state prisons. While users did not have to pay for the tablets, they did have to pay to access much of the content, including books. They were going to be charged .05 cents a minute to read books, all of which came from Project Gutenberg, a free online archive of public domain books.[21]

In response to some of the unfair and exploitative ways tablets have been introduced in prisons, PEN America developed "Best Practices for E-Reader Tablets in Carceral Institutions."[22] Prison book projects and allied organizations have halted other statewide efforts to ban free books in New York, Pennsylvania, and Washington. Despite this progress, the struggle to ensure people's right to read (and receive original mail) is far from over.[23]

The opportunity to read or receive a book can be revoked at any time. Prison book projects across the country share information about restrictions and policy changes regularly; we work together and rely on each other. A book is such a simple offering but after it has navigated the labyrinth of rules and regulations to end up inside a prison, it can mean everything.

Where Are the Books?

"Thank you for the book. And I'm sorry to tell you they would not let me have the book. I really don't know why they won't let me have the book. It's a History book! This place is crazy. I love History books about things like that."

   —Dominic D. Brown

"Our prison library is a travesty, so when I finish these books I donate them to the library here."

   —TN

"Books here are very limited and what good books the library gets usually get stolen (sad but true)."

   —MD

"I can't get a romance book of gay men here. I am hoping you may know someone who could help me."

   —OH

"Thank you so very much for considering my artwork for your book. It honors me greatly. The unfortunate situation for myself at this time is that I am on Maximum Security 24/7 solitary isolation and do not have access to draw or color or create art right now due to the prison's rules. The fortunate situation is that I have reached out to certain people that have some cards that I drew and colored and are going to make 8 x 10 color copies of them so that you will have some of my art to present."

   —Eric Bramblett

"Our library is not worth talking about. Books are an afterthought. It is rare to see a book that is published this year or even last. Most so called new books just have a new book look. The publisher's date are 5–15 years old. We have few of these even. The G.E.D. and library are not coordinated. Rec. Dept sets the library money????? There has been no librarian in 10 years??? Books on trades, computers, science, math, etc., even art are non-existent or outdated beyond use. Few organizations, clubs, churches, and others do more for prisoners than say, 'I wish we could do more.' So when someone such as APBP helps, keeps reaching out and always encourages, is just shut down for what is 'called' security reasons. — Well it sucks. Sure not many prisoners used APBP here but, enough did. I also lost a Christian poetry publisher. This does not only happen at this prison. It is U.S. wide."

—Nelson Graham

"I think that your program ROCKS!! As our book cart is very limited on selections and I would of course donate any books you would send to me right to this jail as soon as I am done with them."

—VA

"Since we are only allowed 6 books in our possession, I started donating them to the library. After a couple months they discontinued accepting donations, but if we received books we were told we could send books home, we pay postage, or we had to exchange books we had previously, and destroy them in order to receive the next book (to keep 6 in possession). What a waste so typical of the DOC. After I informed you of this, several months later, they started accepting donated books again. One for us, yeah!"

—Michael W. Myers

"I am in a fairly new federal prison in WV that does not have many books yet. A lot of us here seem to enjoy reading, so most of the books that our library does have stay checked out."

—WV

"We have no library or library privileges. The only access is to a cart with about 40 torn up, well-used books that are never exchanged."

—VA

"I feel that devices would limit the books available for us to read because there are a lot that aren't available for download, and I'm sure that the devices wouldn't be affordable for all."

—Jason Collins

"I started going to the law library . . . to educate myself about civil law. The problem with the law library was inmates can not check out or take legal books from the law library. I was always distracted at the prison law library and could not get much done in that environment."

—Travis Norwood

"I was told that Ya'll offer free books 2 those who are incarcerated. And if so, I'm very interested in some free books because I don't own a T.V. and you can only get 2 books a week from the prison library."

—Anton'Ari Alexander

"The library cart only comes around once a month and we are only allowed two books. I read a lot and am forced to beg, barter, and swindle books from others to have reading material."

—VA

"Without the support of organizations like yours, we would not have sufficient reading material. I, personally, keep a 'library' of sorts in my room for the ladies in my pod, and when we have all read it, I pass it along via the library cart to help supplement the books, as many (especially the good ones) are so old and worn that they are held together with stickers from our shampoo bottles, etc. and you cannot even see the name on the spine. So essentially, APBP helps keep the sanity, broaden the horizons, and brighten the days of over 1000 people here."

—Sherry Lynn Martin

"This place can give you a constant pounding emotionally and it is hard to be encouraged. I messed up and I have time. They don't really offer anything to learn here (what happened to the college degrees you hear about on the outside?). So why not use my time wisely and pick up something I can use in the real world? So let's start with Math."

—Miles T.

"A friend said I could write you and that maybe you would help me out. I recently started reading and studying the BIBLE and attending church but I had got in trouble and went to the hole and what the guards didn't throw away they gave away all my property including my BIBLE and other study books I had. I have no family or friends to help me and I've asked the guards and chaplain to please get me one, they keep saying they will see what they can find but I'm in the triangle and over here out of sight, out of mind. I was wondering if there was any way you could please send me an original King James Bible and any other religious material so I can get back into reading and learning it. I'm a Free Will Baptist and my cell mate loaned me a little Brown Bible but I have a hard time seeing it because its print is so fine. If you could help me I would greatly appreciate it. I hate to even ask but I'm out of options."

—Charlie

"I received some books from you guys a couple weeks ago and I can't put in words how much that means to me and the other guys here in confinement. I have already read and passed the books along to others that needed them. Our library access is almost nonexistent. Could you send me more to read?"

—TN

"This place doesn't even have a library! Sad but true."

—VA

"I am motivated in learning Criminal Law, why well for one the prison has a somewhat law library, at which I can have access to case citations and the such, and it's a lucrative career in here as well as out there. . . . But the law library only has the books for what the law is not how to learn the law. . . . It took me from 2007 to 2020 to finally find a place that sold Law Student Study Aids books and flashcards . . . but to my dismay the business is moving to the internet, meaning having no more catalogs to look at. The place told me that I had to get the up-to-date prices and stock numbers from the website. I'm like wow how am I to do that when I don't have access to the internet. But my goodness, when I'd looked at this catalog, man it was like being a child at the candy store. I'm like come on really my dream is at my fingertips, but still yet I cannot touch it. But anyway, the books are costly. The crunchtime series and the Emanuel Law Outline series, they are the books I'd love to invest in, only if my prison job would give me the money to buy them with, but that's almost impossible given that I only make $.17¢ per hour."

—James Kelly

Notes

1   See Marie Gottschalk, *Prison and the Gallows*: *The Politics of Mass Incarceration* (Cambridge: Cambridge University Press, 2006), 41–52.

2   Angela Y. Davis, *Are Prisons Obsolete?* (New York: Seven Stories Press, 2003), 26. Also see David Lewis, *From Newgate to Dannemora: The Rise of the Penitentiary in New York, 1796-1848* (Ithaca: Cornell University Press, 1965); Caleb Smith, ed., introduction to *The Life and the Adventures of a Haunted Convict,* by Austin Reed (New York: Modern Library, 2016), xlii–lviii.

3   Douglas Blackmon, *Slavery By Another Name: The Re-Enslavement of Black Americans from the Civil War to World War II* (New York: Doubleday, 2008); *David M. Oshinsky, "Worse than Slavery": Parchman Farm and the Ordeal of Jim Crow Justice* (New York: Free Press, 1996); Talitha L. LeFlouria, *Chained in Silence: Black Women and Convict Labor in the New South* (Chapel Hill: University of North Carolina Press, 2015).

4   Julian Hawthorne, *Subterranean Brotherhood [1914]*, Project Gutenberg, 2012, https://www.gutenberg.org/files/8406/8406-8.txt.

5   Mariame Kaba, "A People's History of Prisons in the United States," *We Do This 'Til We Free Us: Abolitionist Organizing and Transforming Justice* (Chicago: Haymarket Books, 2021), 72.

6   Heather Ann Thompson, *Blood in the Water: The Attica Prison Uprising of 1971 and Its Legacy* (New York: Pantheon Books, 2016); Orisanmi Burton, *Tip of the Spear: Black Radicalism, Prison Repression, and the Long Attica Revolt* (Berkeley: University of California Press, 2023).

7   Peter Wagner and Bernadette Rabuy, "Following the Money of Mass Incarceration," *Prison Policy Initiative,* January 25, 2017, https://www.prisonpolicy.org/reports/money.html; Institute for Justice Research and Development, "The Economic Burden of Incarceration in the United States," *Florida State University*, 2016, https://ijrd.csw.fsu.edu/sites/g/files/upcbnu1766/files/media/images/publication_pdfs/Economic_Burden_of_Incarceration_IJRD072016_0_0.pdf

8   Kathrina Sarah Litchfield, "A Critical Impasse: Literacy Practice in American Prisons and the Future of Transformative Reading" (PhD dissertation, University of Iowa, 2014), 54–55, https://doi.org/10.17077/etd.73bl2olb.

9   Sweeney, *Reading Is My Window*, 20.

10   American Library Association, "Prisoners' Right to Read" (2010), amended in 2014 and 2019, https://www.ala.org/advocacy/intfreedom/librarybill /interpretations/prisonersrightoread.

11   Jeanie Austin et al., "Systemic Oppression and the Contested Ground of Information Access for Incarcerated People," *Open Information Science* 4, no. 1 (2020): 169–85, https://doi.org/10.1515/opis-2020-0013.

12   Christopher Blackwell, "Reading While Incarcerated Saved Me. So Why Are Prisons Banning Books?" *New York Times*, August 17, 2022, https://www .nytimes.com/2022/08/17/opinion/banned-books-prison.html.

13   James Tager, "Literature Locked Up: How Prison Book Restriction Policies Constitute the Nation's Largest Book Ban," *PEN America*, September 2019, 4. https://pen.org/wp-content/uploads/2019/09/literature-locked-up -report-9.24.19.pdf.

14   David Fathi, director of the ACLU National Prison Project, provides a review of censorship policies in "Challenging Prison Reading Restrictions," *American Library Association Intellectual Freedom Blog*, September 28, 2021, https:// www.oif.ala.org/oif/?p=26834&fbclid=IwAR2foqqVZ167xe3H2RDIALB7Lks Dy_NjvXqI8kIcsRKx3tQdrgi3hUeDWW8. Also see Peter Nickeas, "It's the Racial Stuff: Illinois Prison Banned, Removed Books on Black History and Empowerment from Inmate Education Program," *Chicago Tribune,* August 15, 2019, https://www.chicagotribune.com/news/ct-illinois-prison-books -removed-inmate-education-20190815-6xlrmfwmovdxnbc3ohvsx6edgu -story.html; Kendall Harvey, "Censorship in Prison Libraries: Danville and Beyond," *Illinois Library Association,* July 29, 2019, https://www.ila .org/publications/ila-reporter/article/118/censorship-in-prison-libraries -danville-and-beyond; "Banned Books List," *Books to Prisoners,* https://www .bookstoprisoners.net/banned-books-lists.

15   Carileigh Jones, "Thoughts on Censorship and the Sociological Imagination in Prison," *Journal of Higher Education in Prison* 2, no. 1 (2023): 34–38, https://assets-global.website-files.com/5e3dd3cf0b4b54470c8b1be1/648e65 d0712ee49319a8d194_JHEP_V2_Jones.pdf.

16   Christopher Blackwell, "Reading While Incarcerated Saved Me," *New York Times,* April 17, 2022.

17 James Tager, "Literature Locked Up: How Prison Book Restriction Policies Constitute the Nation's Largest Book Ban," *PEN America*, September 2019, 8, https://pen.org/wp-content/uploads/2019/09/literature-locked-up -report-9.24.19.pdf.

18 Leah Wang and Wendy Sawyer, "New Data: State Prisons Are Increasingly Deadly Places," *Prison Policy Initiative*, June 8, 2021, https://www. prisonpolicy.org/blog/2021/06/08/prison_mortality/. Also see E. Ann Carson, "Mortality in State and Federal Prisons, 2001-2018—Statistical Tables," *U.S. Department of Justice*, April 2021, https://bjs.ojp.gov/content /pub/pdf/msfp0118st.pdf.

19 Keri Blakinger and Jolie McCullough, "Texas Prisons Stopped In-Person Visits and Limited Mail. Drugs Got In Anyway," *The Marshall Project*, March 29, 2021, https://www.themarshallproject.org/2021/03/29/texas-prisons -stopped-in-person-visits-and-limited-mail-drugs-got-in-anyway.

20 John J. Lennon, "For Prisoners Like Me, Books are a Lifeline. Don't Cut It," *Guardian*, February 4, 2018, https://www.theguardian.com/commentisfree /2018/feb/04/for-prisoners-like-me-books-are-a-lifeline-dont-cut-it.

21 Valerie Surrett, "The High Costs of Free Prison Tablet Programs," *Books Through Bars: Stories from the Prison Books Movement*, eds. Moira Marquis and Dave "Mac" Marquis (Athens: University of Georgia Press, 2024): 208–222.

22 "Best Practices for E-Reader Tablets in Carceral Institutions," *PEN America*, February 8, 2022, https://pen.org/best-practices-for-e-reader-tablets-in -carceral-institutions/.

23 See Freedom to Learn Campaign https://www.freedom-to-learn.net/; Jeanie Austin, *Library Services and Incarceration: Recognizing Barriers, Strengthening Access* (Chicago: ALA Neal-Schuman, 2021).

Chapter 3

LETTERS AS WINDOWS

*Every prison and jail in Virginia
has a series of cells used for solitary
confinement. Fairfax County
Jail had three units for solitary
confinement. None had windows.*

—Reginald Dwayne Betts[1]

In the restricted space of a prison, many people find that books offer them windows both out into the world and into themselves. In turn, people in prison offer APBP volunteers small windows into their lives through letters. We are often asked to imagine how it feels to be confined, cut off, and separated from the world and those we love. Letter writers express regrets and hopes and intentions. They share poems, memories, and stories about their lives, past and present, and their loved ones. We hear thoughts on local and national elections, on Black Lives Matter, on movements for sexual and gender freedom.

Writers also help us see our region more clearly. In letters, we hear praise for Appalachia, the land and its history. Sometimes people tell of leaving their homeland and their hope to return. But for some, Appalachia offers an alien landscape, nothing like a home.

Central Appalachia is one of the four U.S. regions with the highest concentration of prisons in the country. Tracy Huling notes that

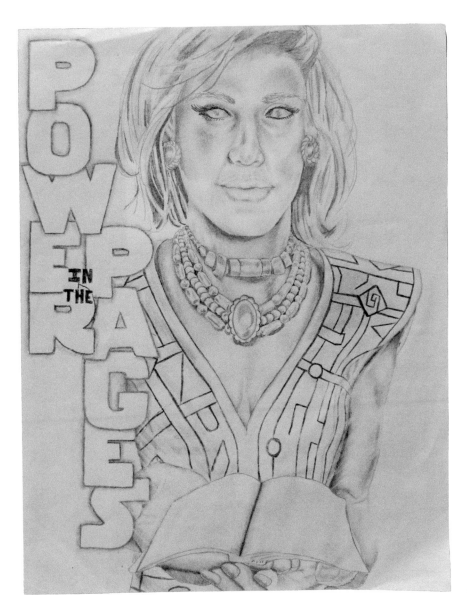

Art by James Jolly

from 1990 to 1999, "245 prisons were built in rural and small town communities—with a prison opening somewhere in rural America every fifteen days."[2] Emma Kelly suggests three primary factors that contribute to the siting of prisons specifically in Appalachia: "the economic vacuum left by the decline of coal, an abundance of open spaces on the landscape left behind as extractive industries have pulled out of our communities, and the cultural marginalization of the region."[3] Many of these prisons are built on mountaintop removal sites exempt from EPA reclamation requirements, and the coal industry has left a legacy of toxic air, water, and soil.

Not only has the prison boom in Appalachia failed to keep its promise of good-paying jobs and economic growth, but considerable damage also follows in its wake. Compared to nonprison counties, many prison counties show higher rates of poverty, lower per capita income, and higher rates of addiction and domestic violence.[4] Transporting people far from their homes disrupts family and social networks and deprives people of the social support so important to their life after release. Further, this practice results in a marked racial disparity between people of color and carceral staff. Peter Wagner and Daniel Kopf report that while Black people are incarcerated at a much higher rate than white people, "prisons are disproportionately located in majority-white areas. This combination has tremendous implications for the prison system's ability to hire appropriate numbers of Black staff, and it gives the problem of prison gerrymandering a distinct veneer of racial discrimination."[5]

Judah Schept and Brett Story argue that the exploitation of this region should be understood within the "broader historical developments of racial capitalism,"[6] as does Nick Szuberla and Amelia Kirby's documentary film *Up the Ridge*.[7] The prison industry's exploitation of Appalachia continues a long-standing pattern of fractured families and social networks: the genocide and land theft perpetrated on Indigenous peoples; the privatization and expropriation of land by speculators and extraction barons; the use of penal law to force involuntary servitude in the mines; today's prisons built on mountaintop removal sites; the profit-making industries surrounding the carceral state; and lobbying for penal policies that truck bodies into prisons.

Schept and Story assert that "Bethlehem Steel, Inland Steel, and other coal companies in Appalachia—and the history of capitalism of which they are a part and which they index—can tell us as much about the carceral state and its vagaries as the changing sentencing laws and attempts at reform that supposedly serve as its barometer."[8]

The state of West Virginia has more people confined in federal prisons per capita than any other state.[9] In general, people in state prisons are incarcerated an average of 100 miles from their previous address, and in the federal prison system, an average of 500 miles.[10] This makes visits with family and friends difficult and sometimes impossible. Phone calls are expensive, and mail is restricted, even though contact with family can help incarcerated people reduce their chances of returning to prison.[11]

The pain of separation is palpable and exacerbated by the infliction of extreme isolation. According to the ASCA-Liman Time-In-Cell report, over 30,000 people are kept in solitary confinement in the federal system,[12] and according to Solitary Watch, the entire carceral system holds about 80,000 people in solitary confinement.[13] Typically this means a person is confined 23 hours a day in their cell; it can be even longer than that, despite the ample evidence of the toll such treatment takes on people's health.[14] "There are many ways to destroy a person," writes Lisa Guenther, "but one of the simplest and most devastating is through solitary confinement."[15] Although some writers, such as Hugh Williams, Jr. in this book's preface and Betts in *A Question of Freedom*,[16] describe solitary as temporary relief, this level of deprivation often causes serious and lasting harm. (In a later essay, Betts writes that he only once considered suicide—while in solitary.[17]) Leonard Peltier refers to solitary as the "most inhuman of tortures. A psychological hell."[18] After years in isolation, Jimmy Santiago Baca found it impossible to speak. The isolation had changed him: "The strain had been too much; I had stepped over that line where a human being has lost more than he can bear." Remarkably, Baca found renewed life through reading and writing. He fell in love with poetry: "When at last I wrote my first words on the page, I felt an island rising beneath my feet like the back of a whale. As more and more words emerged, I could finally rest; I had a place to stand for the first time in my life."[19] Loneliness makes the human connection of a letter and a book especially important.

Many people experience the nearly unspeakable pain of separation from their children, and their regret and worry are expressed in letters. In 2016, 47% of people in state prisons and 57% in federal prisons were parents of young children, and over 5.2 million children have had a parent incarcerated at some point during their lives.[20] Parents in prison are at risk of losing custody if their children are placed in foster care. The Marshall Project completed a study of three million child-welfare cases and concluded: "Mothers and fathers who have a child placed in foster care because they are incarcerated—but who have not been accused of child abuse, neglect, endangerment, or even drug or alcohol use—are more likely to have their parental rights terminated than those who physically or sexually assault their kids."[21]

Children are also in prison. According to the Equal Justice Initiative, about 4,500 children are inside adult prisons and jails, where they face high risk of violence, trauma, and suicide. It remains legal in the United States to condemn children to spend the rest of their lives inside prison, and people prosecuted as children are living out those sentences now.[22] More than half of "emerging adults" in state prison (ages 18–24) are Black or Latinx—an even higher percentage than in the total state prison population. This hyperincarceration of young people of color "is not because they are predisposed to commit more crime; rather, policies and social norms have stacked the deck against communities of color for decades, denying the education and opportunity that often prevents crime."[23] This racial impact extends to adults as well.

In state prisons, Black Americans are imprisoned at a rate that is roughly five times the rate of white Americans, and Latinx individuals are incarcerated at a rate that is 1.3 times the incarceration rate of white people.[24] In fact, every race and ethnicity is overrepresented in prisons, except white and Asian people.[25] In his essay "To Whom the Spirits Toll," letter writer Eddie Hampton Bey states that "there is a social justice war." His life-long experience with the criminal legal system has convinced him that an oppressive and powerful network of forces is deciding "the directions communities such as mine take to go in."

Writers to APBP reveal concern for their physical and mental health. One writer, for instance, let us know that he is not getting his insulin on a regular basis. The most recent national Survey of Prison Inmates reports that state prisons contain a large number of people with poorly treated diseases, disabilities, and/or mental illness.[26] According to Evelyn Patterson and Chris Wildeman, incarcerated people have higher rates of chronic conditions and infectious diseases compared to the general population and that to receive care people must request medical appointments through prison staff and often pay unaffordable fees. The accumulated toll of undermined health and inadequate care impacts people even after release.[27]

The COVID-19 pandemic brought the inadequacy of carceral healthcare into sharp focus. Letter writers communicated their fear, vulnerability, and anger. One told us he felt like "a sitting duck." More than half a million people in the nation's prisons and jails fell sick with COVID-19, and more than 3000 died from it.[28] And yet, despite the significant health threat they faced, many letter writers inquired often about the health of APBP volunteers.

The mental health of incarcerated people is also neglected, with two-thirds not receiving the treatment they need, according to the National Alliance on Mental Illness. And many individuals become entangled in the legal system in the first place because they did not receive adequate mental health services.[29] Prison is traumatic, and incarcerated people are much more likely to have experienced trauma or abuse before entering prison compared to the general population. This makes them disproportionately at risk for post-traumatic stress disorder, depression, and addiction. Very often, prison environments worsen their condition.[30]

Untreated substance use disorder (SUD) is a crisis, especially in jails where overdose is the third leading cause of death. The National Institute on Drug Abuse reports that "an estimated 65% percent of the United States prison population has an active SUD. Another 20% percent did not meet the official criteria for an SUD but were under the influence of drugs or alcohol at the time of their crime."[31] SUD is also a leading cause of death among people released from prison.[32] This alarming mortality rate can be attributed to lost tolerance during periods of abstinence, limited access to medication-assisted treatment and naloxone while incarcerated and when released, and disruptions to healthcare and social supports. These deaths are preventable. Yet only 5% of people with opioid use disorder in jail and prison settings receive medication treatment.[33]

The carceral system also damages the health of those who work inside. The U.S. Department of Justice reported that a variety of stressors pose a serious threat to the mental and physical health of correctional officers and warns that "if not properly managed, stress increases the risk for COs to suffer from heart disease, hypertension, diabetes and a host of other physical ailments. Stress also weighs heavily on guards' mental health and can lead to serious psychological distress, emotional disorders, and an elevated risk of suicide."[34] Appalachia is registering all of this–the economic and environmental impacts, the struggle to provide actual safety and health, and the massive human suffering caused by isolation and despair.

Walls of Isolation

You Can't Imagine
(letter to a past me)

"Can you imagine a world made of concrete and steel,
Where humans bet on the next to be killed?
Can you imagine the sounds of madness, and its screams,
Where no one cares, much less, intervenes?

Can you imagine being lost, and forgotten?
Where saying, 'Out of sight, out of mind' is common, and heard often?
Can you imagine seeing raw hate
Over the color of one's skin, or the complexion of one's face?

Can you imagine being truly alone,
Where no one loves you, and there's no where to call home?
Can you imagine being conditioned in a way
That you ignore others being hurt; where you're programmed to stay out
of their way?

Can you imagine a place where the time stands still
Yet the clock continues to tick on, year after year?
Can you imagine a planet where kindness is perceived
As a weakness, and exploited for another's gain?

Can you imagine being so numb, and dull
That you test the limits of physical pain?

Can you imagine a place where the morals of conduct no longer apply
And most will stay there until they die?

Can you imagine being the remnant of a distant memory
Where you're left out of family's history?
Can you imagine your stories going untold
As your child begins to grow old?

Can you imagine being surrounded by dust and mold
While wiping your nose as it drips from your tears and the cold?
And, as you sit within the walls of your tomb
And the depression starts to loom
While that guilt continues to consume you,
And these memories inside follow you to bed,
Your imagination endorses the war that goes on inside your head . . .

Can you imagine a weapon made of ink and tears,
Where your pen produces sentences in an attempt to neutralize your fears?

Try to imagine that pen as an instrument of peace,
Immersed within the pressure, searching for any release.

Now, awake from that dream, and KNOW that place is REAL.
You should NEVER assume you've won at life's cheap thrills!
See, when you think you have won, you've really lost.
Because, in that world, the gain is hardly ever worth the cost."

   —James Arthur

Prison Life

"It's waiting on letters when you're doing time, And your friends won't write or send a dime. It's waiting on visits that never take place, From friends and loved ones who forgot your face. It's hearing them lie and say they are trying, making you promises but you know they are lying. It's making plans with someone you thought you knew, But their plans suddenly change and they don't include you.

It's hearing them say how much they care, But in your time of need, they are never there. It's hearing their promises that stick in your head, But when push comes to shove, they leave you for dead. It's feelings of love, honor and pride, pain emotions, and hurting inside. It's expressing yourself to your loved ones and friends, But they can't feel your pain because you're in the pen. It's calling and hearing a block on the phone, But you maintain because life goes on. It's really messed up when you're doing time, However, that's prison life, out of sight out of mind."

—Dominic D. Brown

"I'm sorry I burdened you with my sadness. I'll be fine. I'll go watch my friend the spider outside my window. I call him Big Boy because he's pretty big. He cheers me up. I tried to make a call to a lawyer yesterday and couldn't. I haven't used a phone in ten years and they changed how we do it. I'll be glad when Jesus comes."

—Wayne "Gator" Bates

"He will be back in prison was their prediction. And the D.A. don't care, he just wants a conviction. Caught me riding dirty and hit me with all kinds of charges. And I'm in the pen getting write-ups from all the sergeants. I really can't care about what they say, I'm locked up in a cell everyday. They got all sorts of classes for rehabilitation, and they will S.T.G. you by your affiliation. Every day is a struggle to try and maintain, inside this prison with the mentally insane. And everyone you thought would be there for you really ain't. Anyone that you think you can trust, well you can't. Some look at me with hate, and the feeling is mutual. It's a concrete jungle and disrespect. Can turn brutal. It's survival of the fittest, race sticks with race. All of us gets to run, if just some at a different pace."

—Charlie

"I don't have anybody in the free world to help me. My mom passed away 2 yrs ago and now I have a very hard time."

—Backwoods

"Then there's the fact that I've lost my father since I've been In. I should have been there with him to show him I loved him. I should have been beside him when he took his last breath. Instead I've been locked away within these walls, within myself."

—Marc Perelli

"I heard about your Project and I'm so pleased that there is a place like yours. I'm one of the many that don't have anyone on the outside. My mom and dad passed away a long time ago. See I'm 60 years old and there's no one left in my family. All gone. I mean I know people on the outside. But I'm one of those people that just don't feel right to ask someone to help me. There are people in here that make fun of me for not asking for help. I'm just not like that. I will do without before I ask. I put my own self in here. They didn't. God helps me out when I need. And God Bless YOU!!!"

—Steve Rauhuff

"I'm enclosing a copy of an essay I wrote for one of my classes. A letter of apology to someone I hurt, and her reply as I think she would have. (She passed away in November 2016) prior to these writings. Feel free to use them.

I need to apologize to my mother (passed away in 2016 Nov 8th)

I am sorry for having to be away from you at a time when you needed me most of all. I let my worldly desires for success, power, and material things cloud my vision and cause me to stray from the path you tried to keep me on. I let myself fall into deep depression over things that were beyond my control, instead of having faith that God would provide, like you taught me and raised me to do. Now I deeply regret the decisions I made that landed me in this situation and caused me to be apart from you in your time of need.

But now I see clearly, the things you tried to teach me throughout my life, that I should put my faith in God, and know that he has a plan for me to do his work. He has connected me to a group of Christian believers here, and provided me with ample opportunities to worship and praise him. He has given me many opportunities to witness and testify to fellow inmates and staff and I pray for strength and wisdom to carry that out. He has connected me with a group of singers and players that will join me to praise God with music and song. He has instilled in me the knowledge to trust him for everything and let him provide for me for the rest of my life.

So as I finish out my sentence, and after I return home, I will continue to serve him with ministry, praise, and song. Our church family is such a blessing to me still. Like you taught me I know the gift of salvation through Jesus Christ, will bring us together again for eternity in his kingdom. I will see you there mother, and our family circle will once again be unbroken.

With Love, Your Son Michael

Answer to my previous letter

Dear Mike,

I'm sorry you have to be in prison. Hope you are not having too difficult a time. I'm glad you got into the Paws 4 Prison program like you wanted and hope you do well in it. I was glad when you went to the detox and stopped drinking. I wish you had done it sooner, before making so many bad decisions. I know you took good care of me while you could. I hope you will trust in the lord to guide you when you get out and don't fall back into the same traps you were in before. Don't worry about me, I'm doing fine now. Dad says 'Hi'.

I love you
Mom"

—Michael W. Myers

Mom's Home in Heaven

"The cookies Mom used to make,
chocolate chip, peanut butter, and sugar
    cookies too,
she did it with love and caring
Mom loved to bake.
One day Mom got a tumor,
It was in her brain.
She didn't want to be a burden,
The tumor couldn't remain.
Doctors removed the tumor,
The operation was a success,
Then a stroke ensued,
Four months later, she was no more,
She's home with Jesus!"

—Robert D. Fisher

My Life

"I'm like a gypsy in a circus show living my life
    like a rolling stone.
This is how my story unfolds; Traveling man,
    never a home, can't find love so I sleep
    alone.
This whiskey river has a long way to flow,
    where it ends no one will know.
All I know is this life on the road, traveling
    thousands of miles with nowhere to go.
Another day, a few more obstacles to face,
    lights go down, time to turn the page.
Is this all I'm ever destined to be? Life on the
    go, with no family in tow?
I try to drown out all my painful memories,
    and pray to God that nobody sees.
Another long day, now the hours grow small,
    I need another pick me up, before I slip
    down or fall.
There is no one to pick me up, when I slip
    down or fall."

—Charlie

"Now I haven't no money so what I'll do is I'll tell you a story. It's a true story but of course gets bigger with age. I grew up in Balto MD. My mom was a biker chick back in the 60's, she rode, she was in a 16er club, she was a bit twisted, so this story is just her. One day we were picking on my little brother he was about four and wore glasses and my other brother and sister were darker while he was blonde. So we were telling him that we adopted him and that Gypsies left him at our door because they didn't want him, we said we just felt sorry for him and thought he'd make a great pet. Well he started bawling and ran to Momma and told her what we were saying and asked if it was true and he wanted to know where he came from. Momma did the oh no here we go look to the ceiling and then she told him where he came from. She said that the guys that left the big trays of donuts on the porch for us on Sunday morning had left this tray of mixed donuts and we were all sitting and eating them and reading the Sunday paper when she spotted this big fat jelly donut and grabbed it before no one else could. When she bit into it out he popped. :) He thought this was the greatest thing ever. Well a few years later in second grade the teacher was telling the class where babies come from, he said to her that his Momma said he popped out of a jelly donut and his Momma didn't lie to him. He cussed her and everything and was suspended from school and my Momma had to go and tell the principal about the jelly donut theory. :)

Keep the faith,"

—Wayne "Gator" Bates

Appalachia Speaks

"Hello. I grew up just a few miles from the Wears Cove entrance to the Great Smoky Mountain National Park. I love those Appalachian Mountains and spent most of my life enjoying the beautiful views and watching the wildlife play. Thanks for sending me the FoxFire Book. It was a nice book and brought back a lot of memories. My mom would be 93 if she was still living. And she grew up on a small farm in East Tennessee. I was still in grade school when Papaw passed and the family sold the place. I think my mamaw was born in the late 1800s and they still did a lot of the things the book read about. I used to love to hike in the Great Smokeys before a back surgery in Oct. of 2011 put a stop to it. But I know that a lot of the hiking guides told what each trail had in store. And what to look for as you hiked along those paths. . . . I always love the Appalachians. I have seen a lot of them. From Northern GA all the way up to Maine. At least from a car window."

—Anonymous

"Aloha wonderful people
Thank you for the recent books. WV History has produced some colorful people—and heaven-like beauty. Prior to prison, which for me began at 35 years of age, I enjoyed a multi-faceted life. When I left my parents' house in Bucks County, PA at age 18 I never returned except to visit twice. I spent the majority of my life prior to age 35 in both Northern California and the Hawaiian Islands. In 1999 in an effort to sober up (when my wife was killed in 1977 I turned to alcohol for solace), I came East from my cottage in Marin County, California. The last thing that remained in California was an old Harley rat bike. I decided to ride it from California to Virginia, but quite indirectly via a friend in Astoria, Oregon; a friend in Eastern Washington; a couple in Montana; then through Yellowstone; through Nebraska, Iowa, until finally reaching Ohio and getting off the torture of the interstate onto Route 33. When I was getting gas in Elkins I told the chap whose place it was how beautiful WV is. He told me to turn right on Rt 219 that it'd lead to Rt 64 East and VA. I did as he suggested and slowly rode through Pocahontas County, falling in love with West Virginia."

—Jake

APPaLacHiANSSPEAKS?!

Low Valleys & Mountain Peaks! Jagged Edges As
THE Silence speaks! Rocky Terrain as WE
Turn Pages oF our Pain! Reading Between the
LiNES oF the Story, while Being trapped,
Trying NoT 2 Go INSanE! Trying 2 RE-
RIGHT THE Past, So That "Hour" Presence &
FUTure will Be Bright Like the SoN, AFter
The rain! & Even with The Strain, we don't
Put down THE Book, UNtil we finish the Last
Page! "APBP" Is A Great Stage That
OFFers ME A Place 2 UN/eaSE My FRUST-
RaTIONS & RagE! EyE READ 2 Calm my Nerves,
& WiND Down after EYE Have Had a Bad
Day! & even with all oF my Bad DazE,
Eye Steal Never allow It, Two Lead mE
Astray! Books TEach you, how 2 pray! ANd
Books INStill Knowledge & INFuSE THE Mind,
oN How 2 HONE Your Negitive ENERGY &
How 2 RemaiN StroNG, WiN you fill 2 WEEK
Too Be Brave!?...

        WRITTEN:
            BY: ANToN'Ari   Alexander
                    1185995

Writing by Anton'Ari Alexander
(requested to include prison ID
number)

"The system changed. There were so many younger people. You know the juveniles, these people closed down most of their juvenile facilities & sent their juveniles to the adult prison system. And away went the term Reform & Rehabilitation mentality. And now it is all warehousing people. Completely gone is the purpose of prisons! . . . Now, when I first came in this system there were 4 adult prisons. Now there are 40! Can you imagine that. They are filled with kids, children. I am not kidding ya! Sad. But true. Most of them aren't even criminals. They are suspects. But they carry them thru the judicial levels & lock them up! Most of them are poor & uneducated. They don't know anything, except for, what they think is thug shit, they run with it. Most of their sentences are either long & really ridiculous, or somewhat short . . .

I was a soldier on this soil. I had no choice when they threw me out of school because at a young age, I refuse to 'Pledge Allegiance' to the flag. Especially when I knew that the flag wasn't gonna protect me when the police sic their dogs on me or they turn their water hoses on me. I hadn't done anything for them to do that to me, except for my being Black. Yeah, I was a soldier, and very comradish. When they threw me out of school, they got me a job in the cemetery, they thought I wasn't gonna show up to work. But I did. I was a young grave digger! They didn't want me in the school waking up the other students to the truth of things. So they kick me out! . . .

Especially my being young, poor, & Black. I felt this certain way of hope & finding my knack. But, I kept running across Hate & it seems that most white folks were part of a conspiracy to make themselves feel better by hating Black folks . . .

There was plenty of civil disorder among Blacks, so they eased drugs into the picture. From all levels, the government to local police and politicians! Everybody had their greedy ass nasty intent in the pot. And the Blacks browns & poor white folks felt the brunt of the distribution of all the substances which were narcotics! They were planning how to bring the movement down. Because we were schooling the neighborhoods how to become independent! I met Malcolm X in the 60s. I have all these memories in my mix. So much goes on in my head. But I keep the fire to myself. Strong Black brothers was on Hit List. Back in the day! They designed the "master plan" to bring the strong Black men down & fast! Heroin & marijuana. They'd use nightly news to criminalize the use of the drugs & the people that use them & sold them. But, they never said or mention who the fuck was bringing those drugs across the waters to the country. When the Black leaders begin to fall & die, the after thoughts on the streets faded like that of fog under the rays of the sun! Yeah, that "Stop & Frisk," later in the 60s a lot of Black leaders started dying. Being killed by law enforcements all across this country. The list was endless for targets they had to get rid of. Times were hard to survive if you were or had any radical thoughts about the system. 68, Martin Luther King, Jr., 69, Bunchy Carter, founder of the Los Angeles chapter Black Panther Party, Fred Hampton of the Chicago Panther Party murdered in 69. Illegal electronic surveillance and let's not forget 'Incarceration,' the main strategy to eliminate the disagreement and the voices."

—Eddie Hampton Bey

"Yes as you can tell I really love to read. I wasn't very good in school so back in the day I took trade school ½ of the school day. The thing I had to do was once I got out of school we all had to sit down and read for at least an hour (I had 2 brothers). I was grown up in the Great Smoky Mountains so anything outside of the mountains I wanted to know about but it didn't happen overnight. I wanted to go hunt and fish with the other boys in the mountains where I lived but once I got to liking it I looked forward to sitting under the trees and disappearing. I don't even know if they have that program RIF anymore. Reading is Fundamental. Thank God for Dolly Parton and her reading program. So yes, books excite me. I just wish I would have followed what they said. And yes, I will truly enjoy this book that you blessed me with."

—"RED" Lambert

Health Concerns

"The books are great. The Diabetic Carb & Cal guide is exactly what I needed. I have found stats on every food we are served here and almost all of the commissary items. It verifies some of the labels we have questions on. The Hollywood Diet Secrets book is great reading and I notice some things in common throughout, most important is they almost all stress logging/journal your food intake. That's what I've been trying to do all along and the Diabetic guide is a big help. I started at 245 pounds and am now down to 187, that's 58 pounds, WOW!"

—Michael W. Myers

"I am in 'the hole' by my own doing. You see, I'm diabetic, this facility made an open-bay pod into a medical pod, they forced all the diabetics to go to pen-bay due to the Coronavirus pandemic. They were taking the most vulnerable prisoners and putting us in community housing. I was in a cell block at the time with my own cell—no celly. They took me out of cell environment and put me in a pod with zero privacy all open living. Less than two feet apart in sleeping arrangements. If that virus got loose in open-bay every person in there would get sick and some no doubt would die. Thanks but no thanks! I'm content being in the hole. I had to encounter several write-ups for refusing housing but once they knew I was serious they stopped writing me up and finally put me on Ad Seg (administrative segregation). I still get good time and I'm able to order commissary. But am still locked up 23 hours a day. Small price to pay is my reasoning."

—John Pierce Lankford

"I would have wrote you sooner but I caught Covid and wanted to wait until I was well again before responding. I was tested for Covid and tested positive and all the prison did was throw me in a quarantine cell til I was better. No medication to help at all except seven cough drops. I'm sure that's more than some people get so I'm just grateful I got better."

—Hugh Williams, Jr.

"I want to thank you for the last book you sent about meditation. It helped me a lot with my meditation, which is important to me at this point of my life. I spend 2 to 4 hours meditating in search of a quiet place I found myself in when I had a stroke and my mind completely shut down on me. . . . Plus, the books you sent pertaining to health and nutrition are absolutely invaluable to me and others. It surprised me every time I read something that I don't know about living healthier. It makes me want to read and learn more because it makes me realize how little I do know."

—Bob C.

"I would compare prisons' response to this ordeal to someone getting into a car accident and then deciding to put on their seatbelt. They only recently started taking the necessary precautions. None of these safeguards, however, address the elephant in the room. There are a ton of sick and elderly. Fact: these people will die if they are infected. A friend of mine works in the infirmary. He told me that the infirmary simply lacks the ability to care for these people, both in respect to equipment and to personnel. They'll essentially be left in their cell to fend for themselves. Isn't there such a thing as a manual ventilator? I'd be willing to sit and pump air all day. I've been asking some of the men if they wanted me to prepare commutation or compassionate release papers for them. Many know this could end badly. There's really no other way of looking at it.

After all this is said and done, society needs to have a real discussion about the manner in which it wants to punish. If super viruses are the new norm, prisons simply cannot exist in their present form. They're a public health hazard. They are essentially stationary cruise ships. An argument can be made that because these prisons cannot care for those they imprison, their existence is in violation of the Eighth Amendment."

—Steven Lazar[35]

"Thank you for your card notifying me that you won't be sending books as a preventative measure in order not to take the slightest chance of contributing in any way to a single life lost on earth to the coronavirus."

—Bob C.

"Currently we are being locked down for 23 ½ hours a day due to Coronavirus oncerns. We are only allowed out of our cells for 30 minutes each day to shower, make phone calls, and such. I can assure you these books will not go to waste. I plan to forward them to others here and then give them to the library when every-one is done."

— Alan Williams

"Thanks again for sending a book recently. 'The Hood' looks very interesting and already has a lot of guys that want to read it when I finish. The book came at a perfect time; I had just been tested positive for COVID-19 for the 2nd time, making this the 3rd time I have been placed in medical isolation. It is beyond ridiculous here. The folks on the *Titanic* had it better; it was over for them one way or another in less than 4 hrs with fewer deck chair re-arrangements. And the last was wise enough to go down with the ship!"

— Warren Anderson

"I hope the team and families of APBP are well and in high-spirits as we push through this COVID-19 virus together, one day at a time. I believe we will see it through to a thing of the past, merrily forgotten and will only make us stronger as a nation that conquered and destroyed together. Got to have faith!"

— R. Braunschweig

"Let me tell you what's up my way. I had my Birthday on the 4th of September, and my son's Birthday is the 28th of this month too. And we was on Lock-down, and this young guy overdosed but this time he didn't come back because he died. He was only 21 years old, he had a 4 year sentence. He had only been Lock-up for 1 year on his 4 year, and he had made parole last month, and was going home in 3 days. That's the 6th one I have seen die in here. He overdosed on heroin with fentanyl in it. I don't understand at all. Why would you buy something that you KNOW that can kill you? . . . I am 'SCARED' of them Drugs because I have seen what it do to the People that I Love, and care about. It's SAD what happened. He was a really good kid. He just had a problem with heroin."

—Dominic D. Brown

"Because of narcotics my life has changed drastically. Before I knew it everything was catastrophic. I used to get bent way past comprehension, calling the landlord each month, sir, I need an extension. I pissed everything I once had down the toilet. Meth and crack, of course my veins were always full of it. Criminals and junkies is what I associated with. Always trying to hustle up money to get my next fix. You can't begin to know what I mean if you've never shot up before. I wish I would have kept walking when someone showed me that door."

—Charlie

"Almost a decade has passed since I've been imprisoned for my crimes. But I was imprisoned long before by my addiction and I know that was so out of control with my addiction that if I wasn't put away I would have been buried instead. I know from the first time I used heroin, I'd found the next love of my life. I eventually began to sell to keep myself high and unsick. Along the way I've met people who were just like me. They really cared about the state of their lives but were too afraid to admit they had a problem. I've also met some that couldn't care less if I'd die as long as they had my money or product in their hands. But I still wanted to be around them because I got what I needed."

—Marc A. Perrelli

Aspirations

"Hey! What's good your way? How have you been? I hope and pray that you and your family are fine, safe. I talked to the counselor this week and she said that I am done with my time at the end of 2020 around this time next year. And I can't wait to get some home cooked food. I go up for parole 11-14-19 but I don't think I will make it tho. I sent them a Letter about why I can't make parole, and what I have to do to make parole. Because every time I go up they make some excuse why I can't go home. I don't have any write-ups. But their excuse is that they need me to get a new program class. I am so sick of this bull and at times I feel like just giving up. That's why I just think about 2020 at the end, you feel me. That's what I keep my mind on, and to stay out of trouble, keep thinking positive, and stay away from negative people. And make new positive relationships with others."

—Dominic D. Brown

"There have been many before me and there will be many more when I'm gone. I won't be remembered after too long. I would like to leave a mark or a lasting impression, from my life to carry on. What that may be is yet to be seen. But if I can help one person not make the same mistakes I've made, then I can feel good about this journey I've been on.

I'm a father first. A son. Been a lover, on the run. But the most important thing for me has been family. I have taken so much from them by doing this time, that I know no matter what I can never get it back. I have stolen many things in my life but the thing that cost the most was the memories and accomplishments. I should have been there for and I'll never forgive myself for that. I can handle without a doubt this sentence. I know I should be locked up for the crimes I committed. And I'm sorry for so much that I've done when I should have been there for the ones I love. They are the ones that have suffered the most. I'm grateful that I've been forgiven when I should have been unwritten. They should have never had to deal with the pain I've caused. It should have been mine and mine alone. They are right there with me. I'm very grateful for their support because without them I am nothing. My mother bless her heart has always stood beside me all the way.

From the time I open my eyes until the end of the day, there is not a day that goes by that I'm not thinking of them, or what to say. I know one day we are going to get it out in the open all that they are feeling. And I'm prepared to look them in the eyes as they really let me have it. And I tell them I deserve it. And that I'm sorry for my sins. Then there's the fact that I've lost my father since I've been in. I should have been there with him to show him I loved him. I should have been beside him when he took his last breath.

Instead I've been locked away within these walls, within myself trying to become something better than the man that I have been. No longer the junky they remember. I need a shot at life again. I'll give myself to all who need me. Especially my family and my friends. I'll always be judged for all I've done. And I'm fine with that because I've put myself in prison for choices made that I'll never make again. But actions speak louder than words. So only way to prove them wrong is to show them that I'm serious about the things I say and do. And I will redeem myself and even if it's just for me, then I'll know that I remained true. Even coming from where I've been. I am truly emotional when I think of the possibilities. Don't know if it's anxiety or fear that I'm embracing. I'm just looking forward to something better than the life I've lived in the past, only time will tell.

I'm counting the seconds until I get my second chance. This is not coming from someone who's trying to manipulate the system. This is from a man who screwed up his life and now I'm waiting for redemption. I'm finally beginning to see the light at the end of the tunnel. I will keep it pushing. When I was 35 years old I was sent to prison and I'll soon be 43. But I have never believed for one moment that I won't come out of here better. And I'm a firm believer that I can accomplish anything as long as I put something different in my mind and heart. I've been longing to be with my family and to share the love I have. And the experiences I've been through not wanting to actually relive them but to never allow myself to forget the darkness I've crawled through to get to the light in my family's eyes."

—Marc A. Perrelli

Art by Eric Bramblett

"I've been blessed by the talents and skills I have and for that I'm very grateful. All my life music and art have gone hand-in-hand for me. My mom is a very talented artist/musician/inventor/creator and a wonderful example. Before being incarcerated my art was nonexistent. By having all the time in the world and not much else to focus on myself I started leaning towards other artists/musicians. By doing that I learned from them how to play and read music, how to tattoo, draw, paint, airbrush, create leatherwork, sew and many other skills and talents that are interesting. Basically I turned myself into a valuable asset which is a survival trait, but also a monetary income. Some libraries have a lot of DIY type of books that help a person to learn new things. Art of all forms are my life and how I live. The art books that were sent to me from APBP impacted my art skills and helped me learn about other points of perspective when drawing which in turn allowed me to be able to explain how drawing and shading come together to create pictures or images to other struggling artists. Art is an expression of self and acts as a release of feelings, thoughts, pain, etc."

—Eric Bramblett

"I am writing to you in concern of my personal life situation. I am caught up in a sea of continuances from the parole board authority down here. I have been in front of the parole board 13 times. And each time they treat me as though it is my first hearing. . . . They leave us old-law guys stuck here in these prisons. Having to Go & Go Go Go before the parole board. Just like *Shawshank Redemption* the movie. But with me live & in living color!"

—Eddie Hampton Bey

"Dear Adolescent Me: Take this advice with you, please read and learn as much as you can. Educate yourself so you can become a better person than I was able to become. If you apply yourself a little, you might graduate from high school. If you apply yourself enough, you'll earn a college degree like I am. If you apply yourself a lot, you might not be earning that college degree while you're incarcerated in a prison cell. Make better decisions, take the time to learn how to be better than me."

—Todd

"I am 53 years old and been married and divorced two times. I am currently serving a short prison term for some trouble in those mountains. And I learnt in a prison program called Cognitive Behavioral Intervention Program to stay away from problem areas. So I am praying and trying to plan for my future. I am hoping to change mountain ranges from the Appalachians to the Rocky Mountain area. My plans are to try to find a small piece of land in the Rockies and build a small energy efficient bachelor's cabin and a small greenhouse to grow some vegetables for food."

—Anonymous

"I wish that I can go back in time and make it right. But I can't, the only thing I can do is better myself for the future, and help out my kids. Help them NOT end up like me."

—Dominic D. Brown

Notes

1   Reginald Dwayne Betts, "Only Once I Thought about Suicide," *Yale Law Journal* 125 (January 15, 2016), https://www.yalelawjournal.org/forum/only-once-i-thought-about-suicide.

2   Tracy Huling, "Building a Prison Economy in Rural America," *Invisible Punishment: The Collateral Consequences of Mass Imprisonment*, eds. Marc Mauer and Meda Chesney-Lind (New York: The New Press, 2002), 198.

3   Emma Kelly, "Commentary: The Far-Reaching Effects of the Carceral State on Appalachian Communities," *100 Days in Appalachia*, August 10, 2021, https://www.100daysinappalachia.com/2021/08/commentary-the-far-reaching-effects-of-the-carceral-state-on-appalachian-communities/.

4   Robert Todd Perdue and Kenneth Sanchagrin, "Imprisoning Appalachia: The Socio-Economic Impacts of Prison Development," *Journal of Appalachian Studies* 22, no.2 (October 2016): 210–223.

5   Peter Wagner and Daniel Kopf, "The Racial Geography of Mass Incarceration," *Prison Policy Initiative*, July 2015, https://www.prisonpolicy.org/racialgeography/report.html.

6   Judah Schept and Brett Story, "Against Punishment: Centering Work, Wages and Uneven Development in Mapping the Carceral State," *Social Justice* 45, no. 4 (2018): 12. See also Judah Schept, *Coal, Cages, and Crises: The Prison Economy in Central Appalachia* (New York: New York University Press, 2022).

7   *Up the Ridge*, directed by Nick Szuberla and Amelia Kirby (2006, Whiteburg, KY: Appalshop), https://appalshop.org/shop/up-the-ridge.

8   Judah Schept and Brett Story, "Against Punishment," 10. See also Judah Schept, *Coal, Cages, Crisis: The Rise of the Prison Economy in Central Appalachia* (New York: New York University Press, 2022).

9   Peter Wagner, "Why is West Virginia the Federal Prison Capital of the Country?" *Prison Policy Initiative*, June 10, 2014, https://www.prisonpolicy.org/blog/2014/06/10/wv-prison-capital/.

10   Nancy G. La Vigne, "The Cost of Keeping Prisoners Hundreds of Miles from Home," *Urban Institute*, February 3, 2014, https://www.urban.org/urban-wire/cost-keeping-prisoners-hundreds-miles-home.

11   Leah Wang, "Research Roundup: The Positive Impacts of Family Contact for Incarcerated People and Their Families," *Prison Policy Initiative*, December 21, 2021, https://www.prisonpolicy.org/blog/2021/12/21/family_contact/.

12   Arthur Liman Center for Public Interest Law at Yale Law School, "Time-In-Cell: A 2021 Snapshot of Restrictive Housing Based on a Nationwide Survey of U.S. Prison Systems," August 24, 2022, https://law.yale.edu/centers-workshops/arthur-liman-center-public-interest-law/liman-center-publications/time-cell-2021#:~:text=Time%2DIn%2DCell%202021%20is,are%20housed%20under%20these%20conditions.

13   Solitary Watch, "FAQ: What is Solitary Confinement?" revised June 2023, https://solitarywatch.org/facts/faq/.

14   Craig Haney, "Mental Health Issues in Long-Term Solitary and 'Supermax' Confinement," *Crime & Delinquency* 49, no.1 (2006): 124–25. Also see Hans Toch, foreword in *Prison Madness: The Mental Health Crisis Behind Bars and What We Must Do About It*, by Terry A. Kupers (San Francisco: Jossey-Bass Press, 1999), ix–xiv.

15   Lisa Guenther, *Solitary Confinement: Social Death and Its Afterlives* (Minneapolis: University of Minnesota Press, 2013), xi.

16   Reginald Dwayne Betts, *A Question of Freedom* (New York: Penguin, 2010), 164).

17   Reginald Dwayne Betts, "Only Once I Thought of Suicide," *Yale Law Journal* 125 (January 15, 2016).

18   Leonard Peltier, *Prison Writings: My Life Is My Sundance* (New York: St. Martin's Press, 2000), 5.

19   Baca, *Doing Time,* 103.

20   Nazgol Ghandnoosh, Emma Stammen, and Kevin Muhitch, "Parents in Prison," *The Sentencing Project*, November 17, 2021, https://www.sentencingproject.org/policy-brief/parents-in-prison/. For more on children with incarcerated parents, see Lisa Gordon, ed., *Contemporary Research and Analysis on the Children of Prisoners: Invisible Children* (Newcastle: Cambridge Scholars Publishing, 2018); Batya Y. Rubenstein, "Socioeconomic Barriers to Child Contact with Incarcerated Parents," *Justice Quarterly* 38, no.4 (2021): 725–51.

21   Eli Hager and Anna Flagg, "How Incarcerated Parents are Losing Their Children Forever," *The Marshall Project*, December 2, 2018, https://www.themarshallproject.org/2018/12/03/how-incarcerated-parents-are-losing-their-children-forever.

22   Equal Justice Initiative, "Children in Adult Prison," accessed November 2022, https://eji.org/issues/children-in-prison/.

23 Leah Wang et al., "Beyond the Count: A Deep Dive into State Prison
    Populations," *Prison Policy Initiative* (April 2022), https://www.prisonpolicy
    .org/reports/beyondthecount.html.

24 Ashley Nellis, "The Color of Justice: Racial and Ethnic Disparity in
    State Prisons," *The Sentencing Project* (October 2021), https://www
    .sentencingproject.org/app/uploads/2022/08/The-Color-of-Justice
    -Racial-and-Ethnic-Disparity-in-State-Prisons.pdf. Also see E. Ann Carson,
    "Prisoners in 2019," *Bureau of Justice* (Oct 2020), 10. https://bjs.ojp.gov
    /content/pub/pdf/p19.pdf.

25 Wang et al. "Beyond the Count: A Deep Dive into State Prison Populations."
    Prison Policy Initiative, accessed November 2022, https://www.prisonpolicy
    .org/reports/beyondthecount.html.

26 Lauren G. Beatty and Tracy L. Snell, "Survey of Prison Inmates (SPI),"
    Bureau of Justice Statistics (2016), https://bjs.ojp.gov/data-collection/survey
    -prison-inmates-spi.

27 Evelyn J. Patterson and Chris Wildeman, "Mass Imprisonment and the Life
    Course Revisited: Cumulative Years Lost to Incarceration for Working-Age
    White and Black Men," *Social Science Research* 53 (2015): 325–37.

28 The crowd-sourced memorial *Mourning Our Losses* is dedicated to those
    who died while working or confined in prison. Accessed February 4, 2023,
    https://www.mourningourlosses.org/.

29 National Alliance on Mental Illness, "Mental Health Treatment While
    Incarcerated," accessed November 2022, https://www.nami.org/Advocacy
    /Policy-Priorities/Improving-Health/Mental-Health-Treatment-While
    -Incarcerated.

30 Lauren C. Porter, Meghan Kozlowski-Serra, and Hedwig Lee, "Proliferation
    or Adaptation? Differences Across Race and Sex in the Relationship Between
    Time Served in Prison and Mental Health Symptoms," *Social Science &
    Medicine* 276 (May 2021), https://www.sciencedirect.com/science/article
    /abs/pii/S0277953621001477.

31 National Institute on Drug Abuse, "Criminal DrugFacts," accessed November
    2023, https://nida.nih.gov/publications/drugfacts/criminal-justice.

32 Vera Institute of Justice, "Overdose Deaths and Jail Incarceration," accessed
    December 2022, https://www.vera.org/publications/overdose-deaths-and
    -jail-incarceration/national-trends-and-racial-disparities.

33   National Academies of Sciences, Engineering, and Medicine, *Medications for Opioid Use Disorder Save Lives* (Washington, DC: The National Academies Press, 2019), 19–20. https://doi.org/10.17226/25310.

34   Jaime Brower, *Correctional Officer Wellness and Safety Literature Review* (Washington, DC: U.S. Department of Justice Office of Justice Programs Diagnostic Center, 2013), https://s3.amazonaws.com/static.nicic.gov /Public/244831.pdf.

35   Steven Lazar, "'People Will Die': What It's Like to Be in Prison During the Coronavirus Pandemic," *Appalachian Prison Book Project*, April 27, 2020, https://appalachianprisonbookproject.org/2020/04/27/what-its-like-to-be -in-prison-during-the-coronavirus-pandemic.

Chapter 4

CIRCLES, CLASSES, CONVERSATIONS

A grade will never satisfy you.
A certificate will never validate you.
A degree will never cement you.
Education is what happens when you invite a text to a dinner party and
*   then let it help you do the dishes.*

        —Craig Elias[1]

In 2014, APBP created its first book club at a federal prison for women. The group consisted of fifteen inside members and three volunteers. We gathered in a circle every two weeks for two hours. In lively debates, we decided together on what to read. Our first book was Octavia Butler's *Kindred*.

Over the next five years, we read more than 70 novels, plays, collections of poems, short stories, and essays, among them Ernest Gaines's *A Lesson Before Dying*, Michelle Alexander's *The New Jim Crow*, Bryan Stevenson's *Just Mercy*, Zitkala-Sa's *American Indian Stories*, Toni Morrison's *God Help the Child*, Edwidge Danticat's *The*

After taking a literature class, I felt more accountable about everything—my life, my family, the community—but especially accountable for justice. I became more conscious of the world around me.

        —Kevin Burno

Farming of Bones, Julia Alvarez's *In the Time of the Butterflies,* Marjane Satrapi's *Persepolis,* Jhumpa Lahiri's *Unaccustomed Earth,* August Wilson's *Two Trains Running,* Rachel Carson's *Silent Spring,* Kazuo Ishiguro's *Never Let Me Go,* and Leonard Peltier's *Prison Writing: My Life Is My Sun Dance.* We read poetry by Maya Angelou, Langston Hughes, Rainer Maria Rilke, Lucille Clifton, and Nikki Giovanni.

Early on, inside members arrived at our circle with original poems and stories they wanted to share. Soon we were alternating meetings between book discussions and writing workshops. For Celeste, one of the inside members, the reading and writing practice became a healing process: "It was magic in the most simple formula; introduce a space, lay common ground and the result is organic healing." She compared reading a poem by Adrienne Rich to "learning I could mix red with blue to find various shades of purple." After reading "Diving into the Wreck," Celeste said she knew she had "two choices: Explore the wreck, or drown. With the love of the circle and my pencil, I sorted it out."

When we discussed Tony Kushner's play *Homebody/Kabul,* we considered whether travel, as opposed to tourism, might combat racism and ethnocentrism. One person pulled the conversation close and quietly added, "We travel every time we sit down in this circle." Another member, Jeannie, later described book club as "time out of the prison milieu, mentally and spiritually. To the extent possible, we were 'free' from standard prison surroundings, in a room that did not have the feel of barbed wires, guards, uniforms, and oppression."[2]

APBP has launched several more book clubs, each with its own dynamic but based on the same collaborative model. Book clubs are open to those who do not have a GED or high school diploma and to those who may be ineligible for other programs because of sentence length or disciplinary record. A

Art by Terry "Mikey" Kightlinger

wider circle of readers emerges as friends, cellmates, family members, and employees at the prison pick up the most talked-about books. Sarah Jordan Stout, a graduate student at the time, described book club this way:

> When we discussed Kazuo Ishiguro's *Never Let Me Go* in book club, the women leapt into action. They debated characters and plot structure; they posed questions and dove back and forth between book pages and stories from their own lives. Later, prompted by Butler's *Kindred,* we asked one another, "What do we need to pack to survive?" And I realized how these novels, poems, and short stories were transformed in these women's hands into tools—not unlike paper clips and flashlights—to survive in the world. Best yet, as our discussions continued from losses and reunions to activism, buddhism, and police violence, the sense of "us" and "them" melted away. Emerging was a curious, kind, apprehensive, brave, encouraging, funny, wise *we*. Maybe this *we* is the response to our dystopian present. The *we*—like the double heads of playing cards, somersaulting between asking and answering, voices and visions—is our way to survive.

The experience of the book club compelled us to generate more educational opportunities. In 2021, two long-time APBP volunteers cofounded the WVU Higher Education in Prison Initiative (HEPI) and helped to launch an associate degree program inside a state prison. APBP raised money to pay the cost of tuition and supplies for incarcerated students enrolled in WVU courses. Students take courses year-round across a range of subjects, including math, sociology, English, world literature in translation, writing, and history. For Ray, a student in the inaugural cohort of the degree program, "The best part of this journey has been the people I'm on this journey with, and I look forward to every meeting and seeing everyone's face."[3]

College classes in prison can generate hope, direction, purpose, and community.[4] Students consistently report that classes enable them to grow and be challenged, to develop as scholars, thinkers, citizens, and artists. Brian, another student in the inaugural cohort, wrote the following after taking an American drama course:

> Prior to this class, I always kept myself busy with empty achievements. I never read a book and thought critically about it or wrote a paper. Since this class has started, I've begun to take a different approach in my daily life. I now use critical thinking with purpose to better myself and help others when the opportunity presents itself. . . . Not only have I learned a lot about myself, I have written my first analytical paper, I wrote dialogue for a play and failed miserably in my first debate, although enjoyable. I've had my ah-ha moment when I was writing my first paper. In high school when I thought that I was wasting my time, well, I wasted my time chasing everything but an education. This class has allowed me the opportunity to achieve a higher education and has been the most enjoyable experience I've had in prison.

The Education Justice Project at the University of Illinois includes as its first measure of success for its college-in-prison program "emancipated humanity."[5] Students in WVU classes confirm this outcome in their feedback. Boymah observed, "For those few hours in class, I didn't see myself as a convicted felon in a prison visiting room. I was a WVU student in a classroom with twenty-nine of my classmates, learning."[6] Ya'iyr explained, "I have been active in the Inside-Out Program for about a year and it has made a sweeping impact on my life. I'm focused now in a way that I've never been before." Steven Lazar, exonerated and released in 2023, offered this reflection:

The wisdom lies within its application, knowledge is merely irrelevant information if you don't apply it.

Art by Ralphie

In 2007 I was sent to prison for a crime I had absolutely nothing to do with. I was sentenced to die in prison. Sixteen years later, however, my innocence was recognized, and I was fully exonerated. For sixteen years I begged for anyone to listen to me. However it wasn't until I was enrolled in the Inside/Out program that I learned how to properly beg. Through the Inside/Out program I was provided with the writing skills to plead my case. If not for those skills I'd still be sitting in that cage. However, the Inside/Out program provided much more. The program showed me how to free my mind even if my body was bound. I'm now applying the skills I've learned through the program in the outside world. I'll be starting work soon at a nonprofit public interest law firm helping to free the innocent. That would not be possible if not for the Inside/Out program.

My life is spectacular today. It's beyond my wildest expectations. Even my problems are a delight. Tickets, taxes, and traffic are all privileged problems I've longed to have for so long. Yet still I have an immense obligation on my shoulders. My life is a voice for all the men still sitting in cages. For those that have given up hope I'd ask you to reconsider.

We are honored to cocreate educational spaces with extraordinary students, thinkers, and artists. This chapter contains a sample of writing by inside members of APBP book clubs and WVU classes. We are incredibly grateful to each person for their willingness to share their work.

A Flicker of Light

Lee

It was unbearably cold the day we sat huddled around the table in the bagel shop just a few blocks away from the federal courthouse in Greensboro, NC. I made small talk among the group of us, in a futile attempt at hiding my nervousness. I wanted to run, but that would mean running from my family, my elderly mom, my home, and my never-ending hope of one day having a "normal life." On my way out of the restaurant, I stopped at a blackboard with the heading, "Things to do before I die." I picked up the chalk and wrote, "To come home to my family." Then I drove the few blocks to the courthouse and surrendered myself to the US Marshall to begin serving my 52-month sentence.

Three years have passed since that fateful day, and I finally am beginning to see a flicker of light in what has otherwise been a very dark place. Anxiety has begun to set in, and my mind is consumed with so many questions. Questions like who will employ me, how will I pay my living expenses, let alone my restitution, and of course, the most important question of all, "What have I learned?"

Before coming to prison, I went online to research what programs were available in the Bureau of Prisons. There was a wide range of programs available online, but when I actually reached the prison, I was so disillusioned. For a number of reasons, the majority of those programs were no longer available. There were some classes, GED and the like, but not much to offer those with a post-graduate education.

I applied for a library privilege, and I began to read. I read a lot of legal fiction, some true crime, a ton of novels, but the reading left a lot to be desired. I wanted to learn more about people like myself, who wound up in situations such as the one I'm currently in, and what I could do to never wind up in this position ever again.

I borrowed a book from one of the ladies in my unit and she invited me to join the book club. She said it was a small group led by West Virginia University professors, but that she would recommend me as a participant since one of the members was going home. I was so happy for this opportunity because idleness had led me to believe that I was in some type of vegetative state from which I was in dire need of a reprieve.

The book club was held in the visiting area, an area that was well-lit, airy, and set apart from the noisy common areas of the prison. It was a quiet and serene atmosphere that on most days was conducive to learning.

I initially came for the books, then for the peace, and the company of outsiders. At times, I even questioned the subject matter of the books. Too much oppression, racism, poverty, sexism, genocide, death penalty, mass incarceration, etc. Too many social problems. I kept an open mind, however, and I kept coming. Even when I became overwhelmed with emotion about some of the things I read, my peers, the facilitators, the visitors, and at times even some of the correctional staff would avail themselves to me and help me to gain a more positive perspective to get through those times.

As I continued to show up, in time it was no longer about books, or programs, or peace. I began to realize that it was about me, and millions of others like me, who never quite understood how they embarked on a course of destruction and were just as clueless as to why they were unable to change.

So again, the question, "What have I learned?" I've learned that the tentacles of poverty are strong and extend much further than many care to admit. However, no amount of whining or bemoaning a historically biased and corrupt system will bring about any positive change. I've learned that we often view the world through the hand we're dealt, that never ever winning can lead to self-loathing, and that all too often, we become our worst oppressors. Many of us end up in prisons, mental institutions, or as drug addicts—or in cemeteries. And many just give up.

Today, however, there will be no giving up. I think back to Bryan Stevenson in *Just Mercy*. Broken. Crying into the night and wanting to give up but continuing to forge ahead, to help one more incarcerated individual. No, I cannot give up. I can accept personal responsibility and not allow outside voices to become inside voices. Besides, my own conviction is much greater than my felony conviction, and in the words of the great Assata Shakur,

If I know anything at all
It's that a wall is just a wall
And nothing more at all
It can be broken down

Transition

Lee

Perspective is everything. For me, it was always the hard way. By trial and error, or by hook or crook. I visualized my transition from my old perspective. All I could imagine was doors repeatedly slamming in my face as I tried to explain away my background, my conviction, or in legalese, my instant offense.

My 22-year-old son met me at the Greyhound bus. He had become a man in the four years that I was gone, and beside him was his pregnant fiancé. I had spent the whole ride wondering what I would do once I got home. But the pained look in my son's eyes settled it for me. I had to make it this time. I could not ever leave my sons again. This time, I had to make it.

I reported to the halfway house and for the most part, it was a very warm and supportive atmosphere. There were on-site case managers, social workers, and employment specialists who were really helpful in meeting my every need. Once I completed my agenda and submitted it to the staff on duty for approval, I was able to go out into the community on my own to seek employment or address other transitional needs. After four weeks, I was approved to go home on supervised release. I still had to submit a weekly agenda, but I did not have to be home before 9:00 p.m.

In six weeks, I landed a job as a psychosocial rehabilitation facilitator for a community-based mental health agency. I went back to the halfway house with my offer letter to report that I had found employment, but what I encountered was a very somber atmosphere. They were very supportive to all the residents, so I found it a little strange that no one paid much attention to my announcement. I later learned from one of the residents that evening that the prison system had terminated their contract with the halfway house, and the residents that were still under supervision would be transferred to another halfway house in another city that was one hour away.

Initially, I was not worried, because I was no longer in the halfway house physically; I was in community custody, therefore, having very limited contact with the halfway house. I only had to turn in my weekly agenda and be in before my 9:00 curfew. I also had to answer two phone calls during the evening but never after 12:00 a.m. But things were not quite the same at the next halfway house.

This halfway house called you all day and all night. If for any reason you were unavailable to pick up the phone, you would be written up and possibly sent back to prison. An app was placed on my phone that would sound a loud piercing beep at least eight times daily. When the beep sounded, you had one minute to open the app and look into the camera inside and recite the five numbers that were on the screen. Oftentimes, the app would not accept the check-in due to glitches in the system, but you had to repeatedly keep doing it until it was successfully submitted, or you would be written up and placed back in the custody of the halfway house or, worse, sent back to prison.

One day a week, I had to report to the facility to submit a random urinalysis. I had no driver's license at the time, and the halfway house was inaccessible by bus. Each week, I had to find a ride there within a few hours after being notified to report. If I could not find a ride there, I was ordered to report back to the halfway house for violating the conditions of my community release. I rode with anybody I could find because I was so desperate. One day, I rode there with a friend of a friend who worked in that same city. I had to catch an Uber back for $65.

This halfway house offered no support, just punishment. My anxiety was through the roof, and I was constantly being threatened and provoked. I was placed back in custody once for missing a phone call at 2:35 a.m. I complained, and they allowed me to return home so that I would not lose my job. A week later, my driver got lost on the return trip home from the urinalysis, and I wound up arriving home 20 minutes later than the time they had allotted for the trip. I called them while on the road and informed them I was lost. It did not stop them from placing me back in the halfway house the next day and holding me in their custody until my supervised community release was over 15 days later.

I did not know what to do at that point, but I knew that I would lose my job if I stayed out of work for two weeks. I was earning decent money by then, because I had completed my peer support specialist training, and I had several clients that I could service after my regular 9–5 job. I could not lose my job. I had resumed responsibility of my home again, and I had $1800.00 per month in bills that I needed to pay.

So, for two weeks, I borrowed a car from a friend, and drove, unlicensed, for two weeks back and forth to work. I knew, if caught, I would lose everything I had worked for. But then again, that was the plan, just not my plan.

I hated that I had allowed the forces of evil to cause me to commit a crime, but I just could not lose again. That halfway house was worse than prison itself. They never even inquired what I would do upon my release. I woke up and signed my release papers and left without even a goodbye. The people in that awful place really tried so hard to defeat me. They helped me though. They helped me to empathize with the freed slaves who were freed only to be subjected to the Jim Crow laws, or the ones down in Texas who were enslaved an additional two years after the Emancipation Proclamation was signed. They helped to reinforce my commitment to stay focused and not allow myself to be locked up again.

I have been home six months. My life is really coming together. I did not have a hard time finding work. My work is fulfilling, and I earn decent money.

My grandchild was born last week, and I was able to show up. As I get better, my son gets better. Our home is coming together. Everyone is working. We are growing separately and as a family. My job is great. I am working on some really great projects, and I am honored to be a trusted employee. I can't appropriately express how wonderful I feel each time I punch the time clock, and I'm reminded that today I count somewhere. I am not only working to improve my own life, I am also improving lives in my community. Today I stand for something much greater than the institutional census. And yes, I now have my driver license.

The Power in Passing It On
Celeste Monet Blair

As I entered prison with a 30-year sentence for conspiring to possess a controlled substance, I felt as if I were dragging a ball and chain into some alternate universe. Surreal, like walking into a very bad dream. I now know that I had a severe case of PTSD at the time of my arrest, and this was only enhanced by my actual apprehension magnified by my first steps into the system. What I remember the most was the disappointment I had in myself. I saw myself as broken beyond repair, shattered with absolutely no will to go on. Relapse had cost me a good life.

One day a woman in my unit invited me to a Book Club. Anything to escape what appeared to me to be much like THE COLISEUM OF ROME sounded good. I love to read and came to find out the Book Club was actually entwined with these amazing writing workshops. I had always been a painter, never a writer, but the circle of kind, down-to-EARTH visitors kept drawing me back. It felt as if I was a dying, wilting plant handed over to a group of loving horticulturists in a secret garden. Everyone I'd known had let me down and now, this group of strangers showed up, week after week, to build me back up.

Years later, I read in the book *Burnout* by Emily and Amelia Nagoski that persons experiencing PTSD were likely to experience POST TRAUMATIC GROWTH. This included both a better sense of personal strength and appreciation of life. The authors' theory is that one must find the "something larger" which lies within. When I read this, I instantly recognized that this is what the APBP Book Club had given me the space to find. With each meeting, each time I entered the magic circle, I would slowly find my strength. As I began to form a new narrative, I began to heal.

It was magic in the most simple formula; introduce a space, lay common ground, and the result is organic healing. For one, each encounter was serendipitous, and that is how I knew it was real.

When they introduced me to the author and poet, Adrienne Rich, it was like learning I could mix red with blue to find various shades of purple. We read a poem called "Diving into the Wreck." Having been an avid diver, this piqued my interest. As I read the words, this perfect, parallel universe appeared in my mind. Hers was an account of a person, literally diving into the water to explore some bit of wreckage. Something I've done many times with my daddy or some other strong man . . . Ms. Rich said she was going it alone. This notion caused the words on the page to line up with visions so real that suddenly I could see, this poem at this moment, was me in prison. I realized I had two choices: Explore the wreck, or drown. With the love of the circle and my pencil, I sorted it out.

So much time has passed. I've long since transferred to another prison. It took me two years to get permission to facilitate a book club here! We are scheduled to begin mid-summer. In the meantime, I've been teaching creative writing. And when I introduce the women to Adrienne Rich and "Diving into the Wreck," I ask them to apply a COMPARE AND CONTRAST to their own life. I am always amazed by the discoveries they make, but most importantly, we all recognize that none of us are doing it alone.

Art by Celeste Monet Blair, drawing in response to "Diving Into the Wreck"

Open Books

Ya'iyr

To those who dared to look in
and took in
the true stories that are written between the bookends
and discovered a new genre
that explores deep beyond the
stereotypical depiction of monsters
I applaud ya
To those who kept turning the page
who went beyond the bars
and sat down in a cage
I'm amazed
I expected to be unfazed
by some babes
who just learned to walk
but they came to stand by my grave
on Wednesdays
So I'm amazed
that after the horror stories of those days
when I got shot and got stabbed and I got grazed
and I did worse
I heard a judge say a word that left me dazed
then I heard a cry
I turned around & said "mom, it's okay"
Somehow I'm still amazed
by what I found on your page
and how it affected my days
(not just on Wednesdays)
And it feels kinda absurd
That I almost curved
without viewing the cover

before seeing a word
or even reading a blurb
we all need to be heard
and deserve to be read
and the scenes that you crafted
impacted my head
and awakened from slumber
something that I thought was dead
and I'm amazed

bioluminescence

Ya'iyr

we the wretched receive
no respite
we revolve living forever
in revolt some revolution yet
we wither daily and b
y generations rather than
bloom a new creation
folded in frustration
hard
cold

i'm studying mechanics so i can know how things work so i can build something
                                                        and destroy something i'm
studying explosives and foundations and structures i'm studying engineering so i
can
know how things stand
                                                        so i can bring them down
                                              so i can make them fall so
i'm studying demolition and making plans
                                                        i'm studying plants and how
they begin in darkness unseen and some are known to burst through cement but
really
they just found a way through the abstraction in the concrete the substance used to
lay foundations

hard

cold

but not impenetrable b

y beauty formerly concealed in dirt which some call soil

rich

dark and filled with nutrients mainly those needed for plant life

         (without which we'd all die)

nitrogen potassium phosphorus (NPK) ingredients (listen on the labels of
fertilizers) used to bake bombs which break foundations & bring down structures
         (we're all made of the same stuff)
         i'm studying seeds

and soil

and fertilizer

and mechanics

and engineering

because we the wretched remain

concealed until

we realize we're rich and

dark

surrounded by everything we need

to break through foundations

to BŁOOM

so i'm studying horticulture and photosynthesis because we don't need to receive

anything we don't need a respite yes we have been surrounded by death which precedes
decomposition which deposits what life is composed of

(we're all made of the same stuff!)

back into the soil which makes it rich in nutrients
we are seeds hidden in darkness
we are surrounded by richness
potential
concealed beneath foundations
which are

hard
cold

so i'm studying warmth
which is found in we
in closeness

(some organisms that grow in darkness make their own light which is called
bioluminescence
recently scientists
have discovered this phenomenon in humans)

i'm studying we the wretched in closeness in darkness surrounded by death how we
are
rich and how we make our light and how we will break through foundations and

destroy

structures

by becoming gardens wild and untended

                              blossoms and trees

tangled together

                              vines and weeds

rooted in richness

from death making

life

light

BOOM

Searching Fingers

Ya'iyr

brushed across my skin
found me near death
amid a coppery aroma

flakes of black blood
caked on shackles
that chew my wrists & ankles

splayed & stretched
bound to a wall
starved beyond pangs
numb to my wounds

nearly comatose dreaming
floating through darkness
beneath waves
vaguely aware — suffocating

heart rate slowing
beat…by…beat
each inhale: salty, metallic, gritty
what my ancestors tasted

Searching fingers
found my lips

and covered them
and pinched my nostrils

hot rage burned away the fog

so i fight with
my whole being
to deny death

to escape the cruel hands
of tyrants
who relish the sight
of my weeping
blood

who drink my skin
and water their fields
with my pain

blind to the truth
which is that my suffering
poisons the harvest
that they feed to their children

So when searching fingers
found me chained in the dark
I bit them off
and ate them

Dear Dwayne Betts
Dorian La'More

Education can free you in ways that you never fully realize until you are in a place that you crave and dream to be free of . . . know that you can understand that better than most people given the time that you spent in prison. I feel you and I are almost mirror images and polar opposites if that makes any sense . . . I came to prison in the early nineties at the heights of the get tough on crime era and the superpredator rhetoric that captivated the American news cycle. I was the poster child of what a dangerous teen looked like . . . In reality, I was a lost kid in search of understanding and a way out of the inner city cycle of poverty that so many black people get trapped in . . . I have been in prison nearly three decades and I have become a totally different person than I was in my youth . . . I plan to be an advocate for criminal justice reform but juvenile justice will be what I focus on . . . I wanted to express my gratitude for your work. I am ready for my second chance and I hope to meet you in the near future.

Let It Go

Kenny Dade

This villanelle is a reflection on a time in my life when I refused to let some of the smallest things go.

In my world, I sometimes see, black and White,
While searching for solutions, in a day,
Self talk, meditation, answers with care.

With knowledge, comes wisdom, where is the LIGHT?
When gravity pulls, and black turns to gray,
In my world, I sometimes see, black and White.

Young and convicted, caught up in the night,
When there's growth, you won't be stuck in your ways,
Self talk, meditation, answers with care.

Up, down, in and out, looking left to right,
Families, friends, leaving in my old age,
In my world, I sometimes see, black and White.

Stubborn ways, can keep the heart, hard on sight,
As I, grow, grow, grow, while light starts to fade,
Self talk, meditation, answers with care.

And I sit here looking, WOW, it's so bright,
Pondering what I've done wrong, in this cage,
In my world, I sometimes see, black and White,
Self talk, meditation, answers with care.

A Feat of Love

Craig Elias

Spend three months redefining justice with Martin Luther King, Ann Pancake, and Bryan Stevenson and you find yourself rethinking the meaning of other words too. Take "love" for example. The Zale's definition demands diamonds. Hallmark says it's cards. My mom expresses it with chocolate chip cookies. I've seen some things this semester that's given me a different take on love.

Love is a van ride over bumpy back roads before the Dunkin Donuts guy is even awake. Love is having the backbone to turn this into a for-credit course mid-semester. Love is processing hundreds of request slips, hounding counselors for vote sheets, prepping call outs, and securing gate passes.

Love is getting your work done early even though you've got four other classes, and you can feel the hot breath of midterms on the nape of your neck.

In his book *True Spirituality*, Chip Ingram said, "Love is giving someone what they need the most when they deserve it the least at great personal cost to yourself." He must've had me in mind. No one deserves to be a part of the Inside-Out program less than I do. I come from a solid family, was educated in a blue-ribbon school district, and was awarded a football scholarship. I scraped all these advantages off my plate and fed them down the garbage disposal. I didn't just get myself kicked out of college (twice)—I got myself kicked out of society . . . forever. In spite of everything I've squandered, you opted to invest in this program and in me. I can't thank you all enough for making a choice that so exemplifies love.

Catalytic love is the heartbeat of Inside-Out. It pumps blood to broken hands, healing and preparing us to continue the work you've started. The only right way to respond to love like this is to make it count. We make it count within this institution by sharing what we've been given with our fellow prisoners. We make it count inside and out by respecting the program and refusing to do any-thing that might jeopardize it for others. We make it count forever by catching the Inside-Out vision of costly love and making it our own.

Inside-Out is a snowball being pushed up a hill. The bigger it gets the more work it takes to keep it going. So if you value the love we've shared together and if you want your world to be rich and meaningful like this more often, you'll find a way to put a hand on the snowball and do some pushing.

Inside Voicd

Craig Elias
in association with A.Bomb

During the first year of the Coronavirus pandemic, Craig Elias kept a daily journal to document the sudden changes taking place. Here is a short excerpt from his 800-page manuscript.

In the Beginning

A.Bomb is the first person I heard say coronavirus. It was some time in December. He binges *Ancient Aliens* and the *UnXplained* and I assumed the coronavirus was a plague that wiped out some pharaohs or something. So when he said coronavirus I tuned him out.

Inquiring minds want to know what pandemics are like in prison. Today is March 20th—the first day of Spring. I'll try to rewind the best I can and you can walk through Covid-19 with me.

March 5th

Reading a book called *White Fragility*. Interrupting racism is a form of seeking justice. I can already tell it's going to be a full time job. These are the things that occupy my mind, not a red orb with protruding suction cups bouncing through Chinese provinces.

March 13th

A memo shimmied through my cell door. Visits were canceled. Outside volunteers were prohibited from entering the facility. The commissary order limit was increased from $70 to $100. Two weeks was the timeline cited on the memo but anyone watching the news had to think this was just a starting point.

I ended up talking to my mom later in the day. I emailed a half dozen people telling them not to waste their gas driving down here. After that it was business as usual. A friend and I got together for a conference with God. We prayed for Mrs. H and the others on our list. He made a point to pray for The Powers That Be and everyone here . . .

Not everyone was holding up as well as we were. My friend, for example, struggles with depression. The news that the volunteers were no longer welcome in the prison turned him quiet, downcast. We walked to chow together and he told me he was hurting. It takes a lot of strength for a man to say something like that to another man around here. I listened with my ears but not with my heart. I wanted to tell him to toughen up. I wanted to tell him that shit was about to get real ugly and not seeing volunteers for a little while was the least of our problems. I kept my mouth shut and that was good. Minimizing his pain would only have hurt my friend more. But standing in the dinner line I was thinking more about myself than anyone else. Perhaps the reason I wasn't so shaken about the missing volunteers was because I'm visited so regularly by family and friends. I get mail. I make calls. I get emails. My friend gets far less than I do.

This viral journey of suffering had just begun and already I failed to show the love of Christ. It wouldn't be the last time.

March 21st

12:35 p.m. ANNOUNCEMENT: Count time on the Alpha. You have been advised to wear your masks at all times when exiting the cell.

12:41 p.m. ANNOUNCEMENT: Count time on Bravo. Wearing your masks is not mandatory, but we've been advised to tell you to wear your masks.

12:53 p.m. I take a black Sharpie and draw a Ninja Turtle's sneering grin on mine. Raphael has always been my favorite.

May 28th

J is the most loyal friend I've ever known.

This was our first face-to-face in almost a decade. The booth feels like it's a hundred degrees. My chest, my pits, and my back are like a baby's freshly wetted diaper. On one hand it's exhilarating to see him. On the other, our interaction feels contrived. 6 minutes into the chat, the call was dropped. I started thinking The Powers That Be turned out the lights because J's not on my officially approved visiting list. I tapped my foot in the booth until I couldn't stand waiting any longer. I got up and stood next to the wooden bench in the waiting area for what felt like the time it takes an ant to dash 40 yards. We finally got the Zoom reconnected and I spent the rest of the meeting worrying about being watched. I was ultraconscious that my every word and facial expression was being taped. I couldn't be "in the moment" with J. The whole experience was exhausting and I hated it.

I just want to be able to sit with my friend and have the conversations that he and I need to have; to talk about things that only he and I will ever be able to discuss.

May 30th

6 p.m. Y read from the journal last night. Finish was at 1 a.m. He stops at our door during his Extended Toy Run to talk writing, protests, and life. His face is cloth-covered from the cheekbones down. When he mentions George Floyd's murder I pay close attention to his eyes. His pupils dilate when he describes the cop's knee crushing Floyd's windpipe. They narrow when he says what watching another someone who looks like him get choked to death makes him want to do. His eyes are moist as he laments how hard it is, especially during times like this, to navigate what to say and how to say it and who to say it to. There is a deprivation of voice that comes with being black. Talk too softly and nobody hears you. Talk too loud and offended White girls call scared White cops on their cell phones. It's constricting to be black, like having a knee on your throat. It dawns on me while he's talking that "I can't breathe" is more than a slogan about a recent lynching; it's a commentary on American history. Y blinks back tears as he describes his longing for the day that snuffing out black life won't be considered so damn normal. He blinks not at all when he acknowledges the road ahead will be littered with bodies, black and otherwise.

June 22nd

2:17 a.m.

Yyyeeeaaannh!   Yyyeeeaaannh!   Yyyeeeaaannh!
The fire alarm pierced my dream.

Yyyeeeaaannh!   Yyyeeeaaannh!   Yyyeeeaaannh!

It won't stop.

Yyyeeeaaannh!   Yyyeeeaaannh!   Yyyeeeaaannh!

I try to ignore it. . . .

Yyyeeeaaannh!   Yyyeeeaaannh!   Yyyeeeaaannh!

. . . but it's a fire alarm.

Yyyeeeaaannh!   Yyyeeeaaannh!   Yyyeeeaaannh!

My feet slap the cold concrete floor.

Yyyeeeaaannh!   Yyyeeeaaannh!   Yyyeeeaaannh!

I see a guard on the top tier making his rounds.

Yyyeeeaaannh!   Yyyeeeaaannh!   Yyyeeeaaannh!

I'm tempted to yell, "Shut off the alarm, asshole!"

Yyyeeeaaannh!   Yyyeeeaaannh!   Yyyeeeaaannh!

But A.Bomb looks dead in the rack.

Yyyeeeaaannh!   Yyyeeeaaannh!   Yyyeeeaaannh!

I take a leak instead.

Yyyeeeaaannh!   Yyyeeeaaannh!   Yyyeeeaaannh!

The alarm drowns out the flushing.

Yyyeeeaaannh!   Yyyeeeaaannh!   Yyyeeeaaannh!

I crawl back in bed.

Yyyeeeaaannh!   Yyyeeeaaannh!   Yyyeeeaaannh!

It'll be over soon.

Yyyeeeaaannh!   Yyyeeeaaannh!   Yyyeeeaaannh!

It isn't over soon.

Yyyeeeaaannh!   Yyyeeeaaannh!   Yyyeeeaaannh!

I should've grabbed my earplugs.

Yyyeeeaaannh!   Yyyeeeaaannh!   Yyyeeeaaannh!

I lay and wait . . .

Yyyeeeaaannh!   Yyyeeeaaannh!   Yyyeeeaaannh!

. . . and wait . . .

Yyyeeeaaannh!   Yyyeeeaaannh!   Yyyeeeaaannh!

. . . and wait . . .

Yyyeeeaaannh!   Yyyeeeaaannh!   Yyyeeeaaannh!

. . . until it's finished.

9 a.m. Had a fun Zoom debate with two friends about gender roles in the church. One is a complementarian and takes the position that men and women are equal in status but women are subordinate in function. I lean towards the egalitarian side that counters that men and women can only be truly equal in status if you allow them to be equal in function. This is a debate that's gone on in the church forever and not an issue that we ever allow to come between us. The reason I find debating this topic so enjoyable is because my friend is an industrious, outspoken leader and teacher. So while she and her husband verbally espouse their complementarian values, they live in a superbly egalitarian arrangement full of reciprocal love and mutual submission. One day I'll get them to admit it.

July 8th

Upheaval is the name of the game today . . . . [They] unveiled the plan to officially divide the prison in two . . . Each side will have its own set of workers for each job site. I will never again see or serve men who live on three other blocks. Our tiny world, halved

I'm not sure what problems The Powers That Be believe they're solving. I suppose segregation will slow the passing of drugs from one side of the institution to the other and it will limit opportunities for Rivals to fight if these things are their big concerns. But this move seems short-sighted and potentially problematic for a number of reasons. First, it does nothing to address the actual influx of contraband into the institution. We don't make the junk ourselves. It has to be muled in. The Powers That Be have eliminated mail, outside volunteers, and contact visits and guys are still getting toasted. Splitting the jail won't stop the staff members, whoever they are, from visiting both zones with their dope. Secondly, the zone-versus-zone fighting, when it occurs, typically happens at med line and chow. Med line procedures can be altered without changing anything else and chow can be served on the blocks permanently. There have only been a handful of fist fights in certain buildings and other workspaces since this place opened; certainly not enough to warrant an earthquake to our little world. Thirdly, constricting movement and relationships in a place that already feels like living in the center of a noose will choke personal growth and reinforce selfish, individualistic, small-minded modes of thinking. The fewer people we interact with, the more we believe that we are islands unto ourselves and the less others matter to us. Many prisoners are here because we were willing to cheat, rob, kill, and rape who we pleased. The plan should be to help us integrate and associate, not to set up the place in a way that encourages a me-against-the-world mentality. Lastly, the smaller the society that's created, the less like the outside (where the trend is towards globalization) it will be. 90% of the people here are heading home someday. Living in a whittled down, segregated space will make their transition back into the wider world that much more anxiety-inducing. It is yet another needless hardship impeding returning citizens from making a smooth, healthy reentry. And the 10% who are here forever, how will a move like this impact us? Their ability to feel like they're a part of something larger than ourselves, to make a difference, to branch out, to be significant has now been chopped in half. This policy steals the opportunity for purposeful living from a group that has little to spare. Purposeless prisoners do hideous things to staff and inmates alike. The short-term gains The Powers That Be might get by increasing control should've been outweighed by the long-term impact disconnection and fragmentation have on people's health and well-being. To stop some drug passing and fist fighting, the prison is willing to be less effective in its mission to produce men ready and able to safely reenter society and contribute. This new policy is like trying to cut the grass by pushing a riding mower.

July 19th

8:30a.m. *Ca-clack!* My door popped open. "Wake up, guys," a garbage truck voice rumbled. I fumbled for my glasses. A two-man security squad darkened the doorway. Duos like these have been on the block a lot lately. I'm not sure why. Since the corona lockdown was initiated, mass shakedowns have stopped. Sending these smaller teams to hit a handful of cells each shift might be the only way The Powers That Be have decided to conduct cursory contraband checks. Either way, the shakedown boys are in my kitchen bright and early.

I stumbled out of bed and found my mask. A.Bomb zombied out of the cell after me. The guards went to work rifling through paperwork, cabinets, clothes, and boxes. They flipped the pile of laundry at the foot of my bed, dumped my cup of pens on the desk, and didn't find anything worth pestering us about. They called us back into the cell, instructed us to have a nice day, and went on their way. As home invasions go, this wasn't bad. *Thank you, Lord, for protecting us and our property.*

<u>July 21st</u>

9 p.m. Another Weekly Update. We will remain at Level 2 for the foreseeable future. Visits DOC-wide have been suspended indefinitely. Zoom visits end in August. Several additional staff members have tested positive for Covid-19. They will not report back to work until they're cleared. Wear masks. Wash hands. Maintain distance. That is all.

A.Bomb Intel: On TV yesterday someone said to always tell the truth of reality and whatever befalls after it is irrelevant. Or maybe i said that.

Not a Christmas Story

Charles Giordano

It's not snowing, but the air has a crisp feel, the way a week before Christmas should. You and your brother are a pair of dynamos bound into car seats. I am trying not to let my nerves show, as I take you over to your grandparents. I know how this day is going to end; my plan is to have you far away from it.

Your brother, a year older, is already the adventurous one; he loves the idea of tree shopping with Mom-mom and Pops. You are not convinced, especially when I say I'm not coming. I try to explain that I have errands to run and I will pick you up later; you tell me you can help and we can get pizza. I have no answer for a two-year-old's logic, and I'm just not strong enough to send you away. To everyone else you are a quiet child, hardly ever talking. When we are alone, your personality opens up, telling stories and singing along with the TV or radio. As we eat (no way you would forget about pizza) my pager keeps going off. Everyone wants to know if I have heard. With that many people thinking of me, time is even shorter than I thought.

After lunch, your nap instinct kicks in, and I have to carry you from your car seat to the house. Instead of putting you down in your bed, I lay on the couch with you on my chest. It takes about an hour for the phone to ring; there is no one on the other end. Ensuring I am home. Gently I wake you, letting you know it is time to get your brother. Usually you walk to the car, but today I carry you on my shoulders. You love getting a ride up high. You can see everything; everybody can see you. After settling you in, I head for the driver side.

The expected happens quite unexpectedly; the street is no longer empty, and I am in the center of a crowd with everyone yelling. They are screaming at me to get down, I'm screaming that you are in the backseat, and you are screaming over top of everyone for Daddy. It was selfish to keep you with me that day; I justify it by telling myself you are too young to remember. Most mornings I pay for it in that heartbeat between consciousness and open eyes, when my first thought is that the weight on my chest isn't you.

Little Fly
Kevin Burno

As I stand and watch the sun rise and watch it set from the small, rectangular window inside of my 6-x-12 cell, for the first time in my four year bid—while gazing out of the window into the wonderment of the great blue skies—I embrace my imprisonment. My physical confinement.

Each time the sun rises and each time it sets, I experience a new and different awakening. I mostly only go to the window for inspiration for whatever initiative or objective is on my mind at the moment. Somehow, I find a way to block out all the negativity surrounding me. I block out the concrete buildings and the barbed wire fences surrounding the buildings that are in place to help secure my captivity, and I focus on the beautiful scenery of nature: the tall trees that sit up high over the mountains, the great blue skies, the sun as it fades in and out behind the clouds, almost like it's playing peek-a-boo with the Earth, bringing me a much-needed comfort and radiation.

Once I'm defeated by amazement, staring off into the great blue skies, I press my head up against the 5-inch-thick metal bar that stands intact at the center of the small rectangular window (to prevent escaping, I suppose), and I drop my eyes down to the grassy areas below my window. I'm up about two stories looking down, and I zone out into the greenery of the low-cut grass, filled with yellow daisies and dandelions scattered throughout its surface, and all over again, I am consumed by how perfectly coordinated Allah's creation is.

From here, I glance back and forth between the skies and the grassy areas, practically gasping at the pleasure I am receiving from the sight of it all . . .

It's crazy because I remember when I used to laugh whenever I would see a fly trapped inside of my tiny cell. I would watch the small insect fly into the plexiglass window over and over again, buzzing wildly.

Art by Terry "Mikey" Kightlinger

"Flies are so stupid," I would think, watching them try to buzz their way through the plexiglass. After experiencing this episode with the flies many times, I realized it wasn't so funny after all.

I realized that the flies were yearning for nature—for freedom, the outside. The flies were yearning for that beautiful air on the opposite side of the window.

They want out so badly, I imagined, as I watched different flies on different days spend minutes up to hours flying up against the plexiglass, frustrated, trying to get to the other side out into nature.

I soon became aware that I too must feel like those flies. I found myself experiencing truth to the saying, the same things that make you laugh will make you cry.

I no longer think that the flies are trying to buzz their way through the plexiglass. I now get depressed when an episode with the flies happens. I no longer think flies are stupid. I now imagine that the flies feel trapped and want to spread their wings and fly out in the wind, the same feeling I get when I look out my cell window, watching the sun rise and set—but I can't spread my wings and fly yet, because I'm trapped.

Just like the flies . . .

"Just be calm, little fly," I say to myself. "Follow the openings and the cracks, little fly, and they will lead you to the outside . . ."

Blessed up.

Art by R.J. Morin

A Letter to the King
Wayne T. Smith

Dear Dr. Martin Luther King, Jr.,

I was compelled to write to you after having had the opportunity to read your "Letter from Birmingham Jail." It galvanized my spirit and moved me in such a way that it produced a hunger in me to become more acquainted with you and your philosophy.

As a child I was introduced to you and learned of the sacrifice you made on behalf of African-Americans, fighting systemic racism. I had the benefit of hearing you speak with power and conviction concerning racial injustice and the socio-economic issues surrounding African-Americans. Your famous *"I have a dream"* and *"I've been to the mountaintop"* speeches made a black young boy like myself feel a momentary sense of self-worth and royalty within my blood.

I say "momentary" because within an hour of hearing the speeches and being again confronted with the reality of my circumstance, I would go back to feeling worthless, as a speck within the universe. This insecurity was due to my family's social and economic position and the awareness of the same sense of worthlessness within black people all around me.

Why would I have the audacity to believe that I am valued and important if so many people I identified with didn't? Therefore, I felt that I had to come to grips with the fact that although you looked like me, Dr. King, you were different from us—the exception of who blacks were destined to be. This of course made you my hero and birthed within me a great honor and respect for your work and your mission. I admired you, and the sound of your voice always stirred the substance of confidence lying dormant beneath the fear in my soul. Nevertheless, what you referred to in your letter as the "self-respect and sense of somebodyness that blacks have been drained of due to years of oppression" was inherent within me. I was very much aware of it. I hated it so much that I ignored it and sought to repress it. I sought out ways to challenge it with aggressive verbal affirmations about myself to those I thought had noticed it. I tried to hide it with my appearance, believing that decent apparel and good cologne would cover up the stench of insecurity. However, all of these strategies failed. The sense of "nobodyness" was determined to overcome me and had a grip on me that would require a supernatural power to escape.

Afraid to voice that my life felt meaningless, I kept quiet. But I said it as loud as I could in other ways—in my behavior, my character, and my attitude. What frustrated me is that I could not pinpoint when this had started nor why I felt this way. I lacked the necessary skill to identify the root and how to renew this way of thinking.

This dilemma kept me bound. I was not free. But I knew that freedom was my right. You spoke of "the Negro having something within that reminds him of his birthright of freedom." That was true for me, however, like many African Americans, I did not possess the "know-how" to achieve this right. Therefore I channeled this deep longing in unhealthy ways. Nelson Mandela said, "When a man is denied the right to live the life he believes in, he has no choice but to become an outlaw." This to me can be the righteous outlaw as Mandela and yourself, or this can be the criminal outlaw as became the case with myself and is with many young black men across the nation. In reading your letter I realized that many concerns that you held within your heart concerning the black race have come to pass. You expressed your concern for those "complacent negroes who do nothing to fight against racial oppression due to either their low sense of self-worth or their economic security," and you voiced concern for those who out of frustration and despair seek solace in ideologies that promote hatred and bitterness. Neither one of these courses of action produces healthy self-esteem. This is why you called for blacks to stand against injustice in a healthy way—by opposing hatred with love. This concept for many people is a hard concept to grasp.

How can one love the very people who are oppressing, abusing, and hating them? Being the man of faith I have become today, I realize that this mindset is supernatural, spiritual, and godly. It cannot be done in one's own strength, but it has to be a love that proceeds from above. Years ago, as a young boy, I would not have understood this phenomenon. But as a man, one mature in the Christian faith through extensive self-examination and soul investment, I am able to see the world through new lenses. These are the same lenses that I believe you viewed the world through. These are the lenses of God. Now I share your view that love for people (black, brown, white, and yellow) will spring one into productive, effective action; inversely, hatred will move one to destructive, counter-productive action; and complacency will breed stagnation, which in turn leads to deterioration. I am afraid to inform you that it seems as though black people have opted to take the latter two of the three options.

Today, self-hatred and counter-productivity are thriving in black communities. Our fight is no longer directed towards power. Instead, the pent-up frustration of black people has been turned toward one another. There is an epidemic of young black men killing each other with the equivalence of swatting a fly. Because they feel their own lives are meaningless, they believe all black life is meaningless. The hearts of many black young men in America have grown cold and stony. We have cast away the fleshly hearts of compassion. We have forgotten what our fight is against—racism, injustice, and systemic oppression—and have targeted who we should be fighting for. Self-hatred has caused us to hate our own brother. We have ceased being our brother's keeper, and like Cain, have become our brother's murderer.

At the same time, black people are being wrongfully shot down in the streets, targeted, and brutalized by a blue race called police. We are, however, fortunate to have black and white brothers and sisters who have taken the reins in your spirit to stand against this injustice. This is the *Black Lives Matter* movement. Yet still, my heart sighs; because while there are people addressing the black-on-black war, it is not approached with the same fervor as the blue-on-black crisis. In other words, black lives have to matter to black lives first before they will matter to someone else. This is the importance you often intended to stress in your message—that it is paramount that African Americans come to know our worth; that we have value; that our lives have meaning; that we belong here just as much as any other being; that we too are kings and queens; that we have a purpose; and that we were created equal, uniquely crafted by the same master craftsman as all creation. When we acknowledge this, believe it, and walk in it, only then can we reach the mountaintop that you prophesied about so long ago. But too many of us continue to believe the lie that was planted in our ancestors centuries ago and have allowed its roots to grow far too deep and ubiquitously in our hearts.

We miss your presence here because you labored abundantly to attack this root of evil by using your voice to speak the truth in love. Your death left a void in blackness that has not since been filled. Not for the fact that you died (for it is appointed for all men to die), but for the fact that you were murdered—stolen from us by haters, and we are still wounded from its impact. You were our catalyst and our leader, the voice of God for your people as He used Moses to speak on behalf of Israel and pro-claim to Pharaoh "let my people go!" You had no fear in speaking to power although you were powerless, not in the sense that you lacked commu-nal and spiritual authority (in that respect you were powerful), but in the sense that you lacked political and economic resources. The impact you had continues to have a lasting effect on the state of many African Americans and the country today.

We cannot deny that progress is evident. Our presence is more rele-vant in the nation and the world. We have a presence in media, sports, business, academia, entertainment, religion, science, and many other fields. The political arena is much more diverse, and we have been blessed to have had an African American serve as president of the United States. At the same time, it pains me to say we are still very much lagging and have a ways to go. Our presence is overrepresented within the prison and criminal justice system. The black male body is being arrested at exorbi-tant rates. The arrest and sentencing disparities when compared to white males are extreme, to the extent that prison is being referred to as the New Jim Crow—an alternate form of slavery. And indeed it is. As I write this letter to you, I sit as a statistic of another black male convict. Black fathers are being segregated from their homes, creating increased strain on black mothers, and tearing the infrastructure of black families apart. A major reason for this mass incarceration of black bodies is due to the drug called crack/cocaine that devastated African American communities. This drug affected black neighborhoods the way a virus gradually attacks the cells of the body, then rapidly destroys it as it becomes more aggressive with time. This drug, which is ironically a "white" substance, flooded black neighborhoods with the fierceness of a tsunami. Sadly, black people began to benefit from it financially at the expense of poisoning our own people. Crack/cocaine began to corrode black communities from the inside out—an example of the body attacking itself.

The effects of this epidemic are too complex to explain, but they are part of the trap that has been set by the white elite in order to staunch black progress and maintain an American caste system. What angers me is that our people continue to walk into it. Even an animal never walks into a trap that it is aware of. It is true that many black children and teens are uneducated and undereducated, another dilemma critical to the condition of our race. As the voice of the prophet so wisely declared, "my people are destroyed for a lack of knowledge." Many of us are still asleep, content on existing in a fantasy world; and many who are woke do not care to act, for they have accepted their condition as their fate. Nevertheless, by God's grace, there are still laborers of all colors, those who have your spirit; who sacrifice, dedicate their lives, and use their voice and their platform. I have much honor, respect, and love for these living sacrifices. They are needed because racism, prejudice, and discrimination are evils that are very much alive. While some of it is still bold and ugly, a lot of it hides its ugly face behind smiles, professionalism, and political correctness. But we still sense it, see it, and know it.

So, there is still work that needs to be done. The process must start with us individually and collectively taking responsibility for our own actions, completing the soul work necessary to heal, and holding each other accountable. We can acknowledge that there are still people and systems at war against black progress while recognizing that we do not have to be victims of them. We do not have to fall into their snare and play into the hands of the system. The resilience, strength, and fortitude that is in our blood are evident; we started off in this nation as slaves without rights and have risen to positions we could have never imagined. But we have to remember who we are. The ethos that America promotes has caused us to forget.

Due to the patriarchal capitalist mindset we have adopted from this nation, we have begun to equate human value and self-worth with how much money is in our bank accounts. We have not judged our own selves by the contents of our character because we hold the belief that America never has and never will. My heart breaks, Dr. Martin, not just for my people but for all of society. As you once expressed, we are one creation and if one group is affected then the entire world is harmed as a consequence.

By the grace of God, I have awakened out of sleep. I understand my value as a human being, my worth as a child of the most high God, and my royalty as a descendant of kings and queens. I am confident of my ability to affect change on the earth with the influence I have. It may not be in the same capacity or with the same method that you impacted people, but I can do all that I can to honor your legacy and pray that it equates to a lot. I will use my voice to awaken as many sleeping souls as possible. I will speak love's truth and stand for righteousness and justice by getting involved and acting. You once said, "looking away from evil is, in effect, condoning it"—More truth from a wise man.

To be honest, I am still discovering my voice, praying that it becomes louder. Too often I fear that it will be drowned out by gunshots, hand-cuffs, police sirens, jail cells, tears, poverty, war, fear, broken hearts, revelries, envy, greed, and hatred. The sound of evil is very loud. But I hold on to the belief that though love is gentle and quiet, it is more powerful and effective than any other force in the universe. In your letter, you pose a valid question: you ask, "What kind of extremist will we be. Will we be extremists for hate, or will we be extremists for love?" That question pricked my conscience. Hate is not an option for me. Love is the answer. Our world is in desperate need of it. Many frustrated African Americans did not understand your method and rejected the notion of love. I discovered that this love ethic was not your method to begin with, neither was it Gandhi's. God commended His love toward us while we were yet sinners. Love is God's way, and therefore the best way. So I thank you for being an example to the world in love, faith, righteousness, and peace.

Your voice still speaks from heaven with the voice of martyrs. I realize now that although you were a unique figure in history, you were not the exception. You were showing us who we are and what we are capable of accomplishing. You showed us that as people we are all royalty.

With Love and Gratitude, from one King to another.

Wayne

Gotta Get Away

Sean

True story: A grown man pushing thirty willingly read one of those God awful *Twilight* books. Yep. Front to back in every word. Gross. To make matters worse, I *gave* myself to the story. I let some boo-hoo emo teenage romance bullcrap consume my life for a day or two. It's been a secret shame for some time. If my father were alive he'd disown me.

Why on earth would any adult with a sane mind do such a thing? To pass the time in prison! Yes, time in the ol' pokey can trickle by slower than molasses in January. In an effort to escape the boredom of being locked in the bathroom with a miserable stranger, I took the coward's way out and opted to read a coverless book that someone shoved underneath my cell door like some secret document. Still I have no idea who put that book in my cell, but I still curse the hand that injected such trash into my life like I looked him dead in the eye.

"Yo Sean! You did this to yourself!"

Right you are O cosmic narrator, but what you fail to realize is there are good people locked in bathrooms who have no escape from the miserable bore in the bunk below. These poor souls have no outlet, no escape, no sand to bury their heads into. The feet passing by their cell are connected to empty hands which pass no book. That book is a sanctuary, a place where refuge will not be denied. When stranded alone in this world, ink and paper serve as a portal, a gateway to elsewhere. It is my hope that the APBP can be that gateway for those who need to get away.

Our collective … [7]

Skinny Champ Skrilla

A golden circle,
each of us being slight bends in the halo
Each of us, a collection of thoughts
Delicately designed …
Living links in the chain of change
Authors of a new reformation
Abolishers of antiquated thought,
the errors of previous eras
We are participants …
Partakers in progress,
staring down the dilemmas of the world
We inhale and take a silent oath,
an unceremonious pledge
To never become too weary to empathize,
nor too beaten to help
To serve as the better portion of humanity,
giving the gift of us
Sacrificing …
Parts and pieces of ourselves
We, the willing organ donors
Offering our hearts, loaning our minds
as we acknowledge the power of engagement
The beauty of dialogue,
precious invitations into another's world
To sit and commune with living angels
We invite each other in

Whether the furniture is comfortable or ragged,
it feels like home, it is home
For family is what we are
We shall never be blind while in possession of
mind
We know that
vision is a guide even with eyes closed
We remain …
Warriors of will
Some of us flint, some of us steel
Upon our meeting, a spark
Whoosh!
Flames of change emanate from our skin
Look at us …
An assembly of lights,
dancing through the darkness of this world
Standing face to face with injustice
With our hearts fastened by equality,
righteousness will make us bold
It is our human right to intervene
To interrupt injustice while it speaks,
to disrupt during its diatribe
'Excuse us, we have something to say'
If you ever feel weak, draw strength from me,
Draw strength from us,
our strength is in 'we'
We are the Collective

...A LITTLE NOTE...

...A KIND WORD...

...LETTING THE OUTCASTS OF SOCIETY KNOW THAT SOMEONE OUT THERE CARES,

...EVEN IF IT'S JUST ONE HANDWRITTEN SENTENCE AT THE BOTTOM OF A FORM LETTER...

IT MEANS A LOT, AND IT WARMS MY HEART.

THANKS CONNIE.
MUCH LOVE. HANDSHAKE + A HUG.

ALEX THE WULFF

Art and note by Alex-The-Wulff

Reflections on Book Clubs and Classes

"I had to re-think how I teach about the motions of the sky, because the students in my class did not get to go out at night, ever, to see the stars, so instead I focused on the Sun and Moon since those can be seen during the day. It can be a somewhat emotional experience to realize how much I take for granted and to think about how we, as a society, treat people who are incarcerated. . . . They were some of the most eager and devoted students I've ever taught. One student read the book cover to cover the first week, shared with her cell mate, who wrote down questions and saved them for a week until I returned to answer them."

—Kathryn Williamson

"I remember the very first book club we had like it was yesterday. Initially I had butterflies in my stomach because I really didn't know what to expect, because my notion of a Book Club (back then) was something that 'only' women did. But boy was I wrong. I have since discovered that a Book Club is something that 'human beings' do."

—Antonio Oesby

"More than anything, this is a thank you note. Because first and finally, I am grateful for and to each of you. For your time and your courage and your zeal and your hope and your creativity and your determination and unflappable good humor.

Of course, in a perfect world, I would be there to tell you all this in person, but we haven't cracked the code on a perfect world yet, so, as with so many other things this group has encountered, we'll make do with the next best thing. Which, in this case, is a wordy, rambling, passed-along note.

When you read this, I'll be on the road to a conference in New Jersey wishing I was in Pennsylvania. I'm going to present a history paper about tobacco farmers who had to figure out what it meant to be a community beholden to one another and their place even when forces beyond their control tried to tear apart the fabric of their world. I have learned more about that work of determined solidarity from you all than I could ever begin to express. What's more, I'll keep learning from you, even if I won't be seeing you every couple of weeks.

The poet e.e. cummings writes, 'i carry your heart with me(i carry it in my heart)'—I think the carrying of hearts is how we begin to see the world differently. With each of you in mine, the way I encounter the world and the ways I want it to be (which is to say: more just, more free, more full) are forever changed. Thank you for that.

When it's all said and done, the future might be what I'm most grateful to each of you for: utterly floored and thankful for the work you'll do to make your pockets of the world places where all people can flourish.

In hope,
Emily Morrell"

"I feel like I'm helping shape the minds of a generation who may change the world. What I found puzzling is I did not know how institutionalized I was until the WVU students brought life into our classroom. The students are helping remove the institutional stigmas that are associated with prison life. And we're learning together how to break those institutional structures society has made us believe were right."

—Derrick

"One of the more surprising aspects of this class is the esprit de corps between the inside students. Most of us already knew each other a little or at least had a sense about who was who and so on. The sense of camaraderie has helped us become open and willing to help each other out in this endeavor. I don't know if we're aware of it or not, but we all seem to be on a mission of improvement of the self and by proxy an improvement of the opportunities and culture inside these walls."

—Sean

"The only true way forward in this maze of 'rehabilitation' is for both sides to understand each other. The only way to understand each other is to interact—you can't interact if the doors to the prison and your heart are closed."

—Rudy

Notes

1   From 2019 Inside-Out Closing Ceremony booklet.
2   Ryan et al., "Reading and Writing," 236.
3   *WVU Higher Education in Prison Newsletter*, June 2023, https://higheredinprison.wvu
     .edu/news/newsletters/2023/08/03/vol-1-ed-1-2023-june.
4   For research on higher education in prison programs, see Rebecca Ginsburg, ed., *Critical
     Perspectives on Teaching In Prison: Students and Instructors on Pedagogy Behind the Wall*
     (New York: Routledge, 2019); Mneesha Gellman, *Education Behind the Wall: Why and
     How We Teach in Prison* (Waltham: Brandeis University Press, 2022); Daniel Karpowitz,
     College in Prison: Reading in an Age of Mass Incarceration (New Brunswick: Rutgers
     University Press, 2017); Joe Lockard and Sherry Rankins-Roberston, eds., *Prison
     Pedagogies: Learning and Teaching with Imprisoned Writers* (Syracuse: Syracuse University
     Press, 2018). For the return of Pell grants for students in prison, see Charlotte West,
     "They Saw the Demise of Pell. Now Federal Financial Aid is Coming Back," *Open Campus,*
     July 19, 2023, https://college-inside.beehiiv.com/p/saw-demise-pell-grants
     -now-federal-financial-aid-coming-back?utm_source=college-inside.beehiiv.com&utm
     _medium=newsletter&utm_campaign=they-saw-the-demise-of-pell-grants-now-federal
     -financial-aid-is-coming-back.
5   Education Justice Project, "How Should We Measure Success in Prison Higher Education
     Programs?" June 2021, https://educationjustice.net/wp-content/uploads/2022/02
     /One_Pager_-_13_Higher_education_programs.pdf.
6   From 2022 Inside-Out Closing Ceremony booklet.
7   Skinny Champ Skrilla, "Our Collective," *WVU Higher Education in Prison Initiative*,
     accessed November 2023, https://higheredinprison.wvu.edu/research-resources
     /our-collective.

Chapter 5

WEAVING WEBS

*I*n the late 1990s, forest ecologist Suzanne Simard introduced a new paradigm about the nature of forests. In *Finding the Mother Tree,* she describes how trees form "a web of interdependence, linked by a system of underground channels, where they perceive and connect and relate with an ancient intricacy and wisdom that can no longer be denied."[1] Forests, she asserts, are all about relationships, all about how they can feed, protect, and heal each other through their "constant conversations," ongoing exchanges of materials needed for life.

Something like the "wood wide web" of the forest ecosystem, APBP's work participates in a vital interwoven network of community.[2] The exchange of books, letters, and artwork creates a potent channel for connecting people in multiple domains and directions. Book lovers exchange their reading discoveries and joys with each other, inside and out. Letter writers and volunteers offer each other respect and connection while navigating a system that generally creates loneliness and disconnection. People receiving books and respect write about how they are connecting and sharing these resources with each other, creating informal tutorials, mini-libraries, book clubs, and classes (such as the "Underground Book Railroad" that Sweeney heard about from Denise.[3]) Many times, people write about their intentions to give back to APBP or to "pass it forward" when they return to their communities. We once received a kind letter with a six-dollar donation, inviting us to buy ourselves a sandwich. Volunteers unfamiliar with the carceral machine gain knowledge about the criminal legal system, grow through a deeper understanding of the world, and become informed advocates for social justice among their families and communities.

Reaching even farther, when APBP posts requests for books on social media, people are prompted to think about the needs and interests of those in prison. For example, in March 2021, our stock of science fiction and fantasy novels became depleted. When we posted a picture of our empty shelves on social media with a request for donations, within a week we had received five carloads of sci-fi and fantasy books. APBP also connects to the much wider activism network of prison book projects across the country as well as other social justice organizations. It makes us all feel deeply how the love of reading can be a powerful connecting force. This chapter offers a glimpse into the wide variety of connections that this love builds and nurtures.

Community Building

"Thank you so much for the books you sent me. I read them and then shared them with my group. We are passing them around like a bag of chips!"

—WV

"I'm working on a library. You see I took a page from your all's book. The unit that I live in does double duty: the bottom walk has 28 cells and we are in a program called Group Therapy to try and learn how to live life outside of our criminal lifestyles. The top floor has 32 cells and it's called transit cells. It's for people who are just coming to this prison and are waiting to be placed in their cell out on the compound for the duration of their sentences. We get a lot of new people from classification who don't have anything yet except the clothes and stuff to take a shower with that the prison system gives you. Now here is where I take a page from your book. They are locked in a cell 23 hrs a day with nothing so I take the books that you send me and when the guys upstairs get to come out for their hour I let them check out what books I have. There is one thing though, 1 golden rule. I must read every book first. No ifs, ands, or buts about it. So in my own little way by taking a page from your book I try to give back."

—"RED" Lambert

"These materials help me tutor men here at the prison, so anything you send goes towards the development of a group of men."

—TN

"I don't know if our legislators honestly believe that prisons are meant to be places where penitence and rehabilitation are making men out of criminals, but if true rehabilitation is happening it is due to the pure 'want to' of those criminals partnered with the help and encouraging efforts of those like APBP. It is said that all of us have within us two wolves, one good and one evil, battling for our souls. And it is said that the wolf that wins is the one we feed.

Just waking up gives us in prison the ability to have a never-ending buffet of meanness, hate, disappointment, loss, anger, despair, loneliness, etc. But that isn't all, thankfully. I've always believed that I'd have to be dragged away by either angels or demons, fighting to the end. The jury is still out on whether my good virtues outweigh the bad, the only undeniable, uncontested reality is that I have a little say in the matter, and with a very minimal effort, I've reached beyond these four walls with a cry for help.

APBP has been one of the few to answer that call, and with that answer has offered a dose of hope and encouraging support sorely needed in this cold, dark place. Now, with something simple as a book, I can see a world beyond my incarceration, beyond my despair and loneliness. How is this possible? Is it magic? Is it God? I don't believe it is either. No, I believe it is the result of a select few who have discovered that feeding the good inside of themselves provides a nourishing euphoria like nothing else in this world. And maybe . . . just maybe . . . by such an act of selfless good, maybe behind these four walls reconnect to the good wolf inside of them and seek a path that nourishes that good wolf. Not everything we do will change the world, but there are choices we can make to change our world. Let's change our world!"

—Michael Underhill

"You guys are my favorite place to get books from and I am truly happy and lucky to have found you. You guys truly love what you do, and I also believe you value books, read and enjoy them too and understand that a good book can change your life. Am I right? I'm not sure who will read this letter . . . but to whoever opens this and reads it, I want to tell you about an author and his series of books that my mom sent me and have fallen in love with. The author is Richard Phillips, and although he is virtually unheard of, he is now one of my favorite authors. The name of the series is The Rho Agenda, and there are three books in the first set and they need to be read first. Basically it's a science fiction book with some mystery and thriller thrown in and plenty of action. Without giving too much away, the story is about three teenagers who are friends who stumble upon an alien spacecraft in the New Mexico desert in a cave and they enter the spaceship and it basically changes them and enhances them both mentally and physically. The reason I like it is there is a lot of science and physics in the book to explain certain alien technology, but it's described and explained in a way that is easy to follow and makes sense to where it's actually believable. Believe me when I say that once you start reading these books you won't be able to put them down. Anyway, I'm sorry for rambling it's just I don't currently at this time have anything to read because all my books were lost with my property when I was being transported so I hope you don't mind the lengthy letter and I'm very sorry if I have bored you or taken up too much of your time. Also, if you haven't read the *Game of Thrones* books by George R. R. Martin, I hope you get a chance. If there are books that you have read and think I would enjoy and don't have there to send from your book inventory will you please write them down and send them to me when ya'll send the next book to me so that I can have my mom order it for me."

—Robin Mayes

"It is known that the world looks down on some people in prison as being hopeless. Sometimes that makes it hard to request things and actually get a response. APBP shines a light on this by responding to your request with a book and an encouraging letter. This means the world to us. It instills hope. It shows that somebody still believes in us."

—Miles T.

"It's been a roller coaster ride here due to the Cov and as I'm closing in to an end of my sentence I can't wait to keep my pledge of giving back to APBP, plus all the much more to hopefully be part of the APBP team by any means needed. It helps one tremendously to have someone to lean on while being incarcerated, especially with the kindness and compassion of sharing something to read such as a book that some cannot receive elsewise. Thank you again for giving me something to look forward to when I get released and God Bless."

—R. Braunschweig

"You continue to give the gift of both a connection with the outside world as well as the emotional reminder that we are not forgotten."

—James Jolly

"If LeighAnn is around could you please let her know I am thankful for her choice in Italian for me and that I hope her Italian studies are going well?"

—Steven

"I was not sure I would hear from you guys or not but for some reason my heart said relax and calm down they will write trust me and there it was. An envelope with your return address in the top left corner. My heart swelled up like the Grinch's and a smile lit across my face so big I got earwax in the corners of my mouth. I am so sorry that I couldn't stay in touch but my liver has gone sour and the battle to get back on my feet seemed as hard as those battles you read about in those history books. Now ½ way on my feet I got my property back and most everything is gone except for state issue. I sure do miss the days when, with your all's kindness and books, I started that little library. . . . When I got sick I started to collect all the books up to put them in my property and start up again later but I knew that was wrong. The battle I was about to wage tended to lean more along the lines of 'A good battle fought but with only a one way ticket.' So, I followed your lead the day before I left and put out all the books that you guys have sent to me except one. One of you all sent me a book that they said they had read either in school or college about a little knock-kneed feller named *Owen Meany*. I never did get to finish that book (hint hint) . . . I laughed so hard I truly cried. I can't remember when the last time I had laughed, and I don't think I have ever laughed so whole heartedly in my life. It was AMAZING . . . I am in the last year or so of my life from liver cancer and along with that my forgetter is getting better than my rememberer. I don't remember the name of the first book you guys sent me but I'll never forget the kind words that was writ on the request form that came with the book. 'I picked this book just for you. Hope you enjoy it.' Can you imagine someone cared enough for me. Me a knucklehead who has been in and out of these jails, reformatories, prisons, and institutions for 44 years on and off but just for me they stopped what they were doing and dug thru who knows how many books and found a book just for me. I couldn't sing the praises loud enough for the men and women who work for Appalachian Prison Book Project even if I was a 60-pound rooster standing on a hickory stump crowing like the whistle on a runaway train. Thank you guys for all the good times you sent just for me.

Much Luv-n-Respect,

P.S. You know I have never done any good in life, but the night I received your letter saying all that pretty stuff about my writing, I was so proud I crawled into bed with that letter still in my head, and there in the dark, I started crying, because after 60 years I had finally done something that would make my ma and pa proud of me but they are no longer around I had waited too long. Luv you guys."

—"RED" Lambert

"I could have easily let my broken heart heal in a horrible way and wrong way, but I didn't. APBP was truly a special sign with a little serendipity involved because every time I requested a book, APBP always came through for me. I definitely transformed, not only mentally and emotionally but physically as well. I took almost every vice I had, and canceled all negative thoughts and energy and began working out, meditating, and burying my nose in every book I could. . . . Here I had people who never met me, and they are extending their arms to help me. I don't think they realize how serious their impact is on someone like me. Broken hearted with this hole I may never fill, here these strangers were. Sending me books upon request, <u>for free</u>? I wish I could have met some people like you all in the real world that show unconditional love and human empathy without seeing a face to who you're helping in such a priceless way that leaves an unexplainable smile along with a warm feeling that shows me, just because I made a mistake and ended up in prison, not everyone judges me for what I did. At times I thought I would give up, this meditation book APBP sent me, helped in ways I could never thank them enough. APBP most definitely helped me change my life and for that, I am forever in debt."

—Trevor Crawford

"My ultimate goal is to have the ability to create, invent, or innovate tech that can help disabled and elderly people as well as first responders and third world inhabitants."

—TN

"This morning I received your generous gift. If it was not for you I would have no Christmas. It also gives me someone to write to. Having no family, an item in the mail is the only contact with anyone on the other side of this wall."

—OH

"After working adult basic education ⅔ of my time, along with multi-level tutoring in block voluntarily, I asked and was reassigned as a G.E.D. tutor, helping higher scoring students. As with whatever jobs I had in other institutions, I always found tutoring opportunities within the block. From helping to spell for a letter home, math on a commissary sheet, or helping a college student with different aspects of a major grade project."

—Carl E. George ☮

"I assure you these books will not go to waste. I plan to forward them to others here and then give them to the library when everyone is done."

—Alan Williams

"For me personally the APBP has been a blessing in more ways than one and honestly without this resource available to me there is no telling the mindset or position I would be in today. I started using APBP back around 2015 while I was on Max Security, meaning I was confined to a cell 23 hours a day and in there by myself. I didn't have a TV or radio at the time so I could only read books to pass the days. I believe my first book I received was on history plus a dictionary. Included was a little note thanking me of all things. I thought that was just the coolest thing, here are these people who are across the country from me yet cared enough, provided at no cost, and even allowed you to make requests.

I'm from a poor part of Memphis, TN. No one in my family has ever graduated High School or College and never had a decent job. I decided that I may not have money to go to college but I have nothing but time, determination, and with APBP I was gonna teach myself a trade skill that I will have when I'm released. That's what I did. My next request was a Spanish dictionary. This was done for a few reasons, the first being where I live there are a lot of Mexicans. I didn't want a language barrier and second I would be able to translate and help out others in here. I learned the basics on my own and practiced as much as I could with any Mexican. I have been a translator for Mexicans who can't speak English who still have to function in prison. As a result I was given a pay increase because it's considered a skilled job and I've been able to as a result save money and purchase a TV."

—Andrew C. Benson

"I greatly appreciate all you have already assisted me with and want you all to know what you do really does make a difference . . . I will be incarcerated for the rest of my life and I was always down, bitter and felt hopeless. Now I try and find the good in each day and a reason to live and your book project has helped me incredibly."

—TN

"Yeah, we are in jail for breaking the law, and we are doing our time for what we have done, but just because we are locked up that does not mean we are 'scum.' I really think you guys understand that."

—VA

"I don't think you guys realize how much we appreciate what you all do for us! I truly and sincerely want to say thank you for sending us books! For some of us it's the only mail we receive from the outside world. And the books always help someone near + dear to me."

—Yalonda Holt

"To my friend Mrs. Jonna at the Appalachian Prison Book Project,

Thanks for the HA! smiley face, it made me smile."

—Steven

"Last night mail call came to the pod as usual, but unlike most nights, my name was called to receive a package. It was from you at APBP. What many people don't know is mail call and specifically receiving packages is like Christmas. When you receive a book in the mail, the entire pod (regardless of the fact that we don't all usually get along) suddenly comes together saying 'Oh wow! What book did you get?' or 'I want to read that as soon as you're done' or 'Hey, can we read that together in Bible Study?' . . . For that one moment, everyone comes together in fascination over something we take for granted every day when we're free."
—Sherry Lynn Martin

"This is true fack from an inmate named Underwood. I don't mean to bore anyone with my letter, but this is why I want to thank the people at APBP from the bottom of my heart. The only people that can relate to this little note are the people who have 'experienced it their self.' I have spent months at a time in lock up cells at different prisons. The longest I did was 3 straight years. That might sound like nothing but sit in a little prison cell (3 straight years) when time doesn't do nothing but tick by day after day, you find yourself wanting to give up. You cover your cell light up and stay in the dark. Anyone in VA lock up that is reading this kite knows this is true fack. I don't know every thang. But i have been in prison for the past 32 years, and i can say i know it from A to Z when it comes to prison life. I was in one of them dark cells, and a dude spoke to me through a little hole in the wall, asked me if I wanted to read a book. I was too proud to tell him I could not read. I said what the hell yeah man. He sent me a cowboy book. I cut my cell light on and just looked at the words. I asked him where he got the book from. He said a place called Appalachian Prison Book Project. I kept my cell light on that day. And would catch a prison guard doing his checks, and ask him what different words in that book said. I asked the dude beside me if he would give me the address to APBP. It took me two weeks to write that letter. Asking prison guards how to spell different words. But I got it done. I fell back into that old dark side sitting in the dark doing nothing. Then one day the guard opened my cell tray slot and said Underwood I got a book for you. I jumped up and there it was. I said darn they really did answer my request. To make a long boring letter short, I am now sitting in a cell getting ready to take a test dealing with my G.E.D. And I am working in the kitchen (15 hour days). I say to myself I got to this part of my life, with help from people that didn't even know me, so please don't take APBP for granted. That little old book they sent me didn't cost me a penny and it changed my thinking on life. I don't care if this gets printed or not. I just want to thank you all from the bottom of my heart. You all are out there in the free world, could be doing a 1,000 different things instead of sending us a book. Keep up the good work. You all made me feel like a person again."

—Underwood

Volunteers

"It's quite thrilling to do the work of answering book-request letters. Every envelope contains a new challenge and a chance for me to find a way to build a bridge to reach another human being who in many cases is sorely missing the type of normal civil interactions we on the outside take for granted. If I succeed in understanding what the writer is requesting and throw in a few sincere words of kindness along with the book I chose for them, we have both gained.

I feel very fortunate to be able to do this work. In addition to the letters of thanks from imprisoned people (which can be so poignant at times, they've left me speechless), I've also had personal experiences with close acquaintances who have been caught up in our unequal criminal justice system. I know, from them, the importance of maintaining the link to people on the outside who care. It is a true lifeline.

I want to mention how exciting it was for me to come up with a creative way to fill a need in the project. I quickly came to find that many letters contained requests for coloring books. When my aim to get a continual source of coloring books donated fell flat, I decided to search out free images online and print them off in packets. I'm pretty choosy about the content and variety, picking everything from fine art work to adorable monsters to Day of the Dead sugar skulls. I print six packets at a time, so that the content is varied in the event that someone is requesting multiple times."[4]

—Amy Miller

"APBP not only serves incarcerated individuals; they help outsiders come to terms with imprisonment, replacing ignorant stereotypes with the truth of human complexity, and build upon this empathy to encourage support for institutional change that is long overdue.

Still awaiting his trial, my brother calls to discuss Westerns and autobiographies that help him escape the long and solitary hours of maximum security or inspire him to adopt a kinder lifestyle. I trust Tanner's future to the books he reads, and I hope those texts that I have chosen for the bookish individuals who write to APBP, including an unexpected amount of Westerns, will somehow touch their lives or simply help the hours pass."[5]

—Destinee Harper

"Reading letters was humbling and heartbreaking and so human. It wasn't for me to feel good about myself, not something I was doing just so I could tell people about it later. It was just necessary."

—Amanda Witt

"Dear Friend,
I am also an avid lover of classic fiction—you have good literary taste! Both *Pride and Prejudice* and *The Great Gatsby* are among my favorite titles. I hope you enjoy Austen's satirical writing style as much as I do in *Sense and Sensibility*. I also included a composition book for writing purposes. Please feel free to keep requesting once you finish this novel and when you run out of pages! I hear you, I see you, and I wish you health, safety, and happiness."[6]

—Jordan Pugh

"I like to imagine the person reading the book. I like to believe the books are connecting us, a bridge between me and someone I have never met but would like to know."

—Corina Scott

"One of the things that I've learned in my four years as a volunteer at APBP is that a key value of books for people in prison is that they allow them to dream, to imagine other worlds and other lives. This is obviously true of books like novels and histories, of course, but books also allow them to imagine other lives and futures for themselves: becoming a carpenter or starting their own business or even having a self-sustaining farm on a quarter of an acre.

My favorite APBP memory is a perfect example of this. A couple of years ago we would regularly receive requests with long, chatty letters that soon made him a staff favorite. In one letter, he confessed his passion for ham radio and asked if we could send him any books on the topic. Since we didn't have any and it seemed unlikely that we'd get such a specialized book as a regular donation, I put out a call on our Facebook page to see if anyone could help us fulfill his request. We immediately received three different ham radio books from three different donors. Very grateful for their help, we sent them off to him.

In addition, one of our founding members, whose father had been a ham radio enthusiast, gave him a gift subscription to a ham radio magazine in memory of her dad. Because the subscription address was hers but the delivery address was his, the only problem was she had no way of knowing if he was receiving it. And then one day, about nine months later, she got a letter from the magazine saying they had received an article that he had submitted and were considering it for publication. It was at that moment we knew that we were still helping this person to dream."

—Dennis Allen

"In October of 2020, I entered a calming, serene space called the Aull Center as APBP's Outreach and Operations Coordinator. I came into this room as a blank book. In my vocabulary, the terms 'prison' and 'jail' were unfamiliar. My role was more than leading new volunteers, managing the office, or assisting the supervisor of undergraduate students. It was also about education, compassion, and learning the challenges faced by incarcerated individuals in their daily lives.

I am beyond grateful for having such an educative and fulfilling opportunity to complete my internship in this nonprofit organization. There is always something more to learn, something more to do, but now I have the basis to start a change in the criminal justice system. As for today, I can say the blank book I began with is now being written."[7]

—Vanessa Hamade

"Reading books about philosophy is the only thing that got my brother through ten months in jail. I am glad that APBP exists and that I found my way to it."

—Austin Reed

"As I've gotten more into politics and reform in our society, one thing I've wanted to get more involved in is the way that we as a society treat people in prison. When a person goes to prison, they're treated like they're not part of society anymore, and this happens even when people get out of prison. When I discovered APBP, I immediately wanted to get involved. Sending books is something that I didn't realize could be so powerful. I love to read, and it's great that I have the opportunity to send books to other people to encourage them to keep reading."

—Alexus Eudall

"People's names matter. So many incarcerated people write of loneliness, of not having family or correspondence. They express gratitude for our use of their names, as we scribble little notes in the margins of our form letter."[8]

—Maggie Montague

"My job as a facilitator doesn't end when I leave the prison but instead transforms from that of listener into that of messenger. When I tell people about the man in our group obsessed with reading historical romances and Hallmark Christmas stories or about the dad who writes poetry for his daughter, I am consistently met with surprise—surprise that these things don't fit their preconceived notions, surprise at just how human and relatable these men really are.

I learn so much from the men I work with at the Camp. Not just about prison life but about World War II, cars, outdoor survival, magical realism, the Pyramids of Egypt, and so much more. They are all incredibly worldly and seem to have infinite knowledge about certain subjects that keep my co-facilitator and I fascinated and eager to learn more from them. But most importantly, week after week, the group teaches each other about humanity and what it means to be human. Faith, family, loss, love—we talk about these too.

Our conversations are heavy, deep, and meaningful. I will continue to share these and my other favorite anecdotes from the book club with whoever will listen, but ultimately, what I experience when I go to the Camp is indescribable. If I could, I'd tell everyone that they should become a volunteer at a prison. Whether that be as a visitor, a book club facilitator, a teacher, etc., it doesn't matter. What matters is communicating and connecting with those on the inside and breaking down the barriers that stand between us."[9]

—Gabriella Pishotti

Appalachian Prison Book Project

Dear friend,

We have received your letter. After searching through our donations to find the best match for your request, we are excited to send the following book to you.

This book is free and yours to keep. We hope you will enjoy it. Thank you for your request, and please spread the word about our organization.

We can respond to each letter with a maximum of one book and one dictionary or religious text (if requested and available). When your request is filled, you may write us to request another book. We attempt to fill your request as closely as possible. However, please include general areas of interest and genres so we have the best possible chance of finding a book you will enjoy.

We look forward to hearing from you again.

Sincerely,

Appalachian Prison Book Project (APBP)
PO Box 601
Morgantown, WV 26507
appalachianpbp@gmail.com
aprisonbookproject.wordpress.com

Writing by Cody Grey on the
APBP Form Letter

"'Tell me what you read; I will tell you what you are.'

Dear you, all of you—Do you know how beloved you are? Do you know how much we need you as you need us? Every letter, every ask you make, justifies and empowers our existence for another moment, another day, another text. I see and feel you reaching through the bars, the doors, the walls, the hole, the windows, across the green, across the yard, over the peaks and the mountains, following your letters over roads and paths, to land on our desk today. I have opened your letters as well as I can with care. I read and absorb your gratitude, the glimpses of life you share with us, and your curiosities to learn, read, explore more. You ask for dictionaries, thesauri, almanacs, philosophy, religion, literature of all kinds, anything to expand the few feet you're afforded into an imaginative universe abounding, yet still tethered to the rest of us who await you outside. Every letter I read, every book I pick for you, wrap for you, address back to you, I remember walking through similar halls and blocks and yards and looking at the shelves of similar libraries and seeing all the gaps of history, society, thought that you are not afforded for one reason or another. I remember the faces, even if the names are hard to recall, of those like you who made so much use of the books available inside the prison libraries as you make use of the gifts we send back through here, at APBP. To give you these tools, these words, these tomes, and to do whatever we can to avail them to you, is the stuff of our being. I hope you never stop reading, never stop asking us for another word, another page, another volume, until we are all so very free.

    Yours in solidarity, Cody"

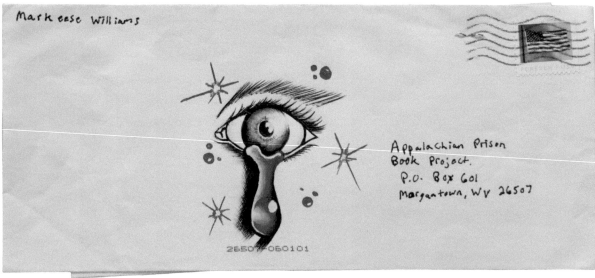

Envelope Art by Markeese Williams

"It's been interesting to interact with folks—not only at the post office but also in my own family—and talk to them about how important the work with APBP is and how it's affected me. Folks at the post office are curious about the packages and where they're being sent to. When a co-volunteer Danielle explained what APBP was and how it worked, other people who were waiting in the line started to ask how to get involved or how to help send books to folks who are incarcerated. Within my own family, I've talked a little about running mail and how important it is to help get folks who are incarcerated reading material. I also had to explain how difficult to understand some of the rules and regulations are at certain prisons and how something as simple as getting a book can require jumping through multiple hoops with packaging and addressing and pen color and tape and etcetera. This mostly surprised them, especially my mom, who's been an English teacher for over twenty years. She seemed a little shocked and sad that reading isn't necessarily a guaranteed right and that some people have to pay *per minute* to read. I want to say that I'm surprised by her not knowing this, but I'm not—the prison industrial complex has worked very hard to make sure that its practices are covered and invisible, especially to the larger public.

I also talked a little bit about my work with my grandma, who wanted to donate books to APBP. (As a side note, she was very unsure about her donations, but for a really funny reason. She asked me, 'Are you sure that these romance novels will be okay? Do they want to read romance novels like this? Are you really sure that they'll request these?' I assured her that yes, folks who wanted romance novels would love to read her donated ones!) Our conversation made me laugh, and it was good just to reassure her, and to say out loud, that people who are incarcerated are still people.

Running the mail and being more involved in APBP has also allowed me to get to know Danielle better, which has been a joy. It's been really nice to learn from Danielle and to get her perspective on things like social justice, restorative practices, and abolitionist movements. She's smart and thoughtful and an amazing abolitionist. Overall, my service to APBP has become such an important part of my life and has encouraged me to ask more questions and try to do more in most of everything that I do. It's also shown me how important it is to help those who are within the prison industrial complex make connections with the outside through letters and books."[10]

—Morgan Roediger

Notes

1   Suzanne Simard, *Finding the Mother Tree: Discovering the Wisdom of the Forest* (New York: Knopf, 2021), 5.

2   For more on ecological approaches to organizing, see adrienne maree brown, *Emergent Strategy* (Chico: AK Press, 2017); Daniel Lim, *Building Regenerative Cultures*, accessed June 26, 2023, https://dlimconsulting.com/regenerativeculture/.

3   Sweeney, *Reading Is My Window*, 55.

4   Miller, Amy. "Appalachian Prison Book Project Fall 2019 Newsletter," *Appalachian Prison Book Project*, October 8, 2019. https://us7.campaign-archive.com/?u=80b64fbbab 78210a17e1b27e0&id=82d928d766.

5   Destinee Harper, "Found between Pages: Volunteering with the Appalachian Prison Book Project," *Moveable Type* No. 9, *1455*, January 2022, https://1455litarts.org /movable-type-issue-no-9-found-between-pages-by-destinee-harper/.

6   Jordan Pugh, "We Will be Here as Long as You are Stuck There," *Appalachian Prison Book Project*, November 4, 2021, https://appalachianprisonbookproject.org/2021/11/04 /we-will-be-here/.

7   Vanessa Hamade, "The First Page," *Appalachian Prison Book Project*, April 8, 2021, https://appalachianprisonbookproject.org/2021/04/08/the-first-page/.

8   Maggie Montague, "Books Make Time Move a Little Faster," *Appalachian Prison Book Project*, April 26, 2018, https://appalachianprisonbookproject.org/2018/04/26/books -make-time-move-a-little-faster/.

9   Gabriella Pishotti, "Lessons from a Prison Book Club Volunteer," *Appalachian Prison Book Project*, January 8, 2020, https://appalachianprisonbookproject.org/2020/01/08 /lessons-from-a-prison-book-club-volunteer/.

10 Morgan Roediger, "What It Takes and What It Means," *Appalachian Prison Book Project*, July 16, 2021, https://appalachianprisonbookproject.org/2021/07/16/what-it-takes -what-it-means/.

WHERE IS THE HONEY?

Darrin Lester

With a third eye and an open mind, I have found connections between honeybees and incarcerated people. Honeybees have been around for 30 million years and have a hard outer shell. Many imprisoned people know how essential a hard-shell mindset is because we are vulnerable to being ridiculed, taken advantage of, and physically assaulted. Although none of us in prison can imagine 30 million years of incarceration, many of us "feel" like we have spent 30 million years inside in a world of concrete, Concertina wire, and steel. And most of society fears being "stung" by people who've been in prison.

I use these analogies to begin a conversation about honey. When most people encounter a bee's nest, they try to avoid it at all costs. The same phenomenon can be said about those incarcerated. There is fear and avoidance. But is there also honey? I think there is a certain sweetness in seeing someone become aware of their potential. There is sweet nectar when one recognizes their own humanity. There is a palate soothing when the taste of transformation begins to take shape in the hearts and minds of a marginalized person who wants to challenge themselves to be better, not bitter, and remove criminal mindsets and assume the power of choice. All the above could be seen as honey. Yet for me, I see this as a product created from honey.

The question remains, "Where is the honey?" When conscientious people on both sides of the fence begin to embrace favorable outcomes, is that not the honey we all want?

The process often begins when a book is opened and read; it becomes the science called pollination and creates the foundation from which transformation is possible. In the same way that beeswax is essential for making honey, an incarcerated person begins to turn pages and opens up the possibilities. Words become the pollen that is carried into the hive or minds of those who can think past immediate circumstances. Readers become engaged in a mental tug-of-war that challenges them to understand the world is much bigger than the neighborhoods they originated from. Add this to the desire to be more than an "inmate, felon, convict." As the words come off page after page, they become the internal incubator that through imagination and realization leads to self-worth and growth. It provides the opportunity to look within and sincerely inspect where they have come from, where they are, and where they hope to be. The heart and soul begin to turn, much like a metamorphosis of a new life.

Makes Me Wanna Holler by Nathan McCall had this effect on me. The author was from my hometown. I could relate to the visual of Cavilier Manor and picture the small colorful homes of Black homeowners who were retired military or worked at the shipyard.

For many Black Americans in the 1950s and 1960s, homeownership was made possible by enlisting. Black navy men were mainly relegated to being cooks and errand boys and sent to segregated beaches, never mind that the ships were anchored in the same water. Owning one of these homes was the feeling of reaching the middle class. These homeowners were proud that military menial jobs could lead to middle-class status. This community gave to those watching the possibility that one day they would be able to cross the red-line barrier of white neighborhoods. The community would never have come about without homeowner loans.

Mr. McCall's writing was like walking through those streets I enjoyed growing up. The memoir was the springboard that made my transformation possible. When I first read the book, I was in the exact prison that housed Mr. McCall. I would challenge myself with the thought that I was on the same ground this brother walked! I followed the principle of education and how it allows for the hope of one day being free from the fear of police arresting me. I learned that being considered a "professional man" was possible. I could be an asset to my community instead of a leech in the community. In all honesty, it planted the seeds of contemplation because, at that point, I was deeply entrenched in criminal behaviors that would open the door to two more incarcerations.

When I came to the end of myself, I went back and read the book again, and it had a deeper meaning because, like Mr. McCall, I was tired, frustrated, and saddened by the pain of lost opportunities and the lost trust of my community, and I was completely sickened by the mess called "my life."

The process that allowed the author to thrive became the blueprint for myself. He rid himself of the crime culture and began to focus on what he wanted to accomplish; he faced his profession courageously with the knowledge that he had to be three times as good as his colleagues because he carried the scarlet letter of a convicted felon. He would be attached to that label forever, and some would be leery of his presence. That was particularly valuable to me because I knew that I would be shunned by some people and refused employment due to cruel policies that prevent licensure and access. I learned to never be afraid to step into a new life because of fear of judgment and failure. People like us have to "knock on more doors" and find that individual who will consider the old person and compare it to the present person and will reflect on all the mountains climbed and rivers crossed. Your talk is illustrated in your walk.

Robert E. Roberts' book *My Soul Said to Me: An Unlikely Journey Behind the Walls of Justice* also had an impact on my life in prison. It was through this book that I wrote the curriculum for Olive Tree, a peer education program. It was an epic breakthrough because I became convinced we had the power to heal each other. The main point was how the men would hold each other accountable and challenge each other to create a better version of themselves. They comforted one another, empowering each other while inspiring themselves to think more profoundly and move cautiously. This was a radical thought for a prison environment. However, I was confident this could be replicated under similar circumstances. After spending eighteen months reading other transformative stories, it was time to experiment with this new philosophical matter of change, and Olive

Tree began. Since then, more than 500 men have graduated from the program. From killers to drug dealers to shot callers, the men signed on to hold each other accountable and support each other in their trials and hard times. The men came to believe they did not need to remain slaves to a system designed to keep them in poverty or prison. I love to see an underdog win.

I do not doubt that this is where the honey is!

AFTERWORD

Steven Lazar

*L*ike many kids, I began reading when I was around seven years old, and depending on the subject, I've always enjoyed the activity. However, I really didn't know how to read until I was in my thirties.

At that point in my life, I was serving a sentence to die in prison for a crime I did not commit. I was in the very final stages of my appeal process, and according to the statistics, I had a 1.8 percent chance of not dying in prison.[1] Not exactly inspiring odds. I knew I was innocent, so I would never stop fighting, but being a logical person, I began grappling with the prospect of dying in a cage. I started calculating my life expectancy, making sure to tally in the fact that each year I spent in prison would take two years off my life.[2] I figured that sometime in my sixties, I'd die a miserable, sad, and painful death surrounded by steel, concrete, and clatter instead of children, grandchildren, and love. I began looking at this life as very temporal and focused my attention on death and The Beyond. I came to grips with the fact that I'd never father children and that not only was my life being vanquished but my future lineage also.

There is a tradition in prison that whenever someone is getting ready to go home, his buddies basically spend the entire day with him walking around the yard and discussing his future. The first meal he wants to eat. The first person he wants to hug. The first exciting activity he wants to do. Other guys would chime in, "Well, I know I'm gonna do first . . ." "Nah, this is what I'm gonna do . . ." When it would become my turn to say something, someone would quickly change the subject, knowing that the notion of "future" wasn't something I was permitted to imagine—my condition was terminal.

I would never be able to buy and decorate a house, own a dog, or jump in a pool again. I would never wear regular clothes again, go grocery shopping, or drive a vehicle. I would never sit in a restaurant and wine and dine with friends; instead, I would eat what I was told to eat and when to eat it. I would never own a piece of property that couldn't be confiscated without any reason whatsoever. I would never sit on a toilet seat again that wasn't made of steel, let alone be able to use the bathroom without another man, probably a stranger, in there with me. My body would never be mine again, and for the rest of my existence, I would be subjected to random strip searches entailing the exploration of body cavities I'd never even seen. For the rest of my life, overweight breaded buffoons called correctional officers would belittle, harass, and torment me, and there wouldn't be a thing I could do about it.

For the remainder of my life, displaying any type of vulnerability would be totally out of the question, and in order to survive, I would have to get comfortable living in a perpetual state of callousness. I'd meet friends in prison and develop relationships that lasted decades, only to find out one day that my friend had been shipped to a different caging facility thousands of miles away and I would never see them again. I would only be able to speak to my family on fifteen-minute, monitored phone calls, and when my loved ones passed away, I would not be able to attend their funerals or give them a farewell hug. I remember one day watching the news and hearing about some famous actor being diagnosed with a fatal illness and only given months to live. I recall becoming involuntarily envious of their condition.

One of my heroines is a tiny Filipino/American journalist/activist named Maria Ressa. Despite her small stature, she has been a fierce advocate of free speech and speaking truth to power. She lived by a motto, "Embrace your fear. Imagine what you're most afraid of. Touch it and hold it, to rob it of its power." I live by those words, and it is in that spirit that I accepted the fact that my life ended when I was 22 years old, that I'd die in prison, and that whoever really committed this crime would never be brought to justice—whatever that means. Worst of all, though, my legacy would falsely go down in the annals of history as that of a murderer, as that of someone who played God and took the life of an innocent person—*that*, however, I would never accept.

It was in this state of mind and state of life that I heard poet Fred Moten guest speak during an Inside-Out literature class. Two weeks before the speech, our class was given Mr. Moten's curriculum vitae, as well as a book of his poems. As I thumbed through his CV, I quickly realized that he was the real deal—professor of performance studies at New York University . . . professor emeritus at the University of

California . . . previously taught at the Universities of Brown, Duke, and Iowa . . . Harvard graduate. Then I opened his book of poems. I guess Moten's poetry would be termed abstract. Yet, I don't think that adjective really does it descriptive justice. Here's a stanza from Moten's poem, "Fugitivity is immanent to the thing but is manifest transversally":

and tear shit up. always a pleasure the banned
deep brown of faces in the otherwise
whack. the cruel disposed won't stand
still. apparatus tear shit up and

After reading Moten's book of poems, my excitement for the speech quickly dwindled. I'm not knocking abstract poetry. It's just not my thing, and if you were to tell me that hearing Mr. Moten speak would change the way I read, write, and even think and feel, I would have told you that you're crazy. But that's exactly what happened. He showed up to class dressed as ordinary as could be imagined and began his speech by saying hello and asking what we wanted to talk about. He talked about being a janitor at one point in his life, and how his son has autism. He was totally relatable. When asked to describe a particular stanza of one of his poems. He pulled out some reading glasses, glanced at the poem, chuckled, and said, "I don't know. Honestly, I don't know what I'm writing half the time. It's just stuff that pops into my mind." I loved this guy!

The dialogue went on in this jovial fashion for a while, until a student asked Mr. Moten what he was currently reading. Soberly, he said, the *Narrative of the Life of Frederick Douglass*. The mood in the room changed as Moten straightened his seating posture. He said that he'd been reading the book for several months. He explained that reading to him was almost spiritual and that words had almost divine attributes and implications. He likened reading to going to church. He said that when he decides to read a book, he becomes totally immersed in the writer's words almost to the point of going into a trance, and it becomes a form of meditation. He tries to totally connect with the writer and to ruminate on each word, the use of the word, the sentence, and the preceding sentence. He said that when we read, we are glancing into reflections of a writer's soul, and that this is a grave and special encounter.

Moten's description of reading had a profound impact on me, and I immediately sent away for a copy of the *Narrative of the Life of Frederick Douglass*. A few months later, I received the relatively short paperback and began devouring it. I can vividly recall this period of my life. My final appeal had just been denied, eviscerating any realistic chance of me not dying in prison an innocent man. I read the book with a heavy and bitter heart, and despite me being a White male, and Frederick Douglass being an African American slave, I never felt a stronger connection to someone's words, particularly read in the spirit of Moten. "I was now about twelve years old, and the thought of being a slave for life began to bear heavily upon my heart." "I often found myself regretting my own existence, and wishing myself dead; and but for the hope of being free, I have no doubt but that I should have killed myself, or done something for which I should have been killed." "The nearest estimate I can give makes me now between twenty-seven and twenty-eight years of age.

I come to this, from hearing my master say, some time during 1835, I was about seventeen years old."[3] To this day, it is my favorite book, and it gives me goosebumps even now thinking about it.

I didn't know it at the time, but Douglass and I would chart similar paths. Douglass should have never been a slave—the word "slave" shouldn't exist—and I should have never been in prison. The word "exoneree" shouldn't exist. In reading Douglass's book, without foreknowledge of his story, you'd have to be pretty optimistic to believe he'd become a free man, let alone a monumental figure in American history. And in reading my story so far, you'd say the same thing. However, three months ago, despite all my appeals being exhausted, new evidence was disclosed of my innocence, and I was fully exonerated, with even the prosecuting attorney demanding my release.

I'd been snatched from the pit of death, the pit of despair, and the hands of a master. Everything I'd said for sixteen years had now been recognized and solidified. I now live in my own apartment with a view of Center City Philadelphia, and I work at the very law firm that helped free me. I am a totally free man. My wounds no longer fester but are painful and grotesque scars. This is the state of mind, state of life, and state of existence that I read the book in your hands. It is in this state of mind that I read Dorian's words: "Education can free you in ways that you never fully realize until you are in a place that you crave and dream to be free of." It is in this state of being that I read Kenny's words, "When gravity pulls, and black turns to gray." It is in this state of wellness that I read Ya'iyr say, "beauty formerly concealed in dirt which some call soil." It is in this state of love that

Craig's words penetrate my soul: "The only right way to respond to love like this is to make it count." My friend, I'm trying.

That's what this book is all about: words and hearts. Allowing words to illuminate a dark place. The Appalachian Prison Book Project is the lighthouse that guides these words.

Notes

1   Carol G. Kaplan, "Habeas Corpus: Federal Review of State Prisoner Petitions," *Bureau of Justice Statistics*, March 1, 1984, https://bjs.ojp.gov/library /publications/habeas-corpus-federal-review-state-prisoner-petitions.

2   Emily Widra, "Incarceration Shortens Life Expectancy," *Prison Policy Initiative*, June 26, 2017, https://www.prisonpolicy.org/blog/2017/06/26 /life_expectancy/.

3   Frederick Douglass, *Narrative of the Life of Frederick Douglass: An American Slave, Written by Himself*, edited by John R. McKivigan, Peter P. Hinks, and Heather L. Kaufman (New Haven: Yale University Press, 2001), 36, 37, 13.

WORKS CITED

Abbott, Jack Henry. *In the Belly of the Beast: Letters from Prison.* New York: Vintage, 1991.

Alexander, Michelle. *The New Jim Crow: Mass Incarceration in the Age of Colorblindness.* New York: New Press, 2010.

Alexander, Patrick Elliot. *From Slave Ship to Supermax: Mass Incarceration, Prisoner Abuse, and the New Neo-Slave Novel.* Philadelphia: Temple University Press, 2016.

American Library Association. "Prisoners' Right to Read." Adopted June 29, 2010, by the ALA Council, amended July 1, 2014, and January 29, 2019. https://www .ala.org/advocacy/intfreedom/librarybill/interpretations/prisonersrightoread.

American Prison Writing Archive. Accessed on May 14, 2024. https://prisonwitness.org.

Austin, Jeanie. *Library Services and Incarceration: Recognizing Barriers, Strengthening Access.* Chicago: ALA Neal-Schuman, 2021.

Austin, Jeanie. "Mail Digitization." March 1, 2021. https://jeanieaustin.com/2021 /03/01/mail-digitization/.

Austin, Jeanie, Melissa Charenko, Michelle Dillon, and Jodi Lincoln. "Systemic Oppression and the Contested Ground of Information Access for Incarcerated

People." *Open Information Science* 4, no. 1 (2020): 169–185. https://doi.org/10.1515/opis-2020-0013.

Baca, Jimmy Santiago. "Coming Into Language." *Doing Time: 25 Years of Prison Writing*, edited by Bell Gale Chevigny. New York: Arcade 2011, 100–108.

Baldwin, James. "An Open Letter to My Sister, Angela Y. Davis," *If They Come in the Morning: Voices of Resistance,* edited by Angela Y. Davis et al. New York: Verso, 2016.

"Banned Books List." *Books to Prisoners*, accessed on January 30, 2023. https://www.bookstoprisoners.net/banned-books-lists.

Beatty, Lauren G., and Tracy L. Snell. "Survey of Prison Inmates (SPI)." *Bureau of Justice Statistics*, 2016. https://bjs.ojp.gov/data-collection/survey-prison-inmates-spi.

"Best Practices for E-Reader Tablets in Carceral Institutions." *PEN America*, February 8, 2022. https://pen.org/best-practices-for-e-reader-tablets-in-carceral-institutions/.

Betts, Reginald Dwayne. "Could an Ex-Con Become an Attorney? I Intended to Find Out." *New York Times Magazine,* October 16, 2018. https://www.nytimes.com/2018/10/16/magazine/felon-attorney-crime-yale-law.html.

Betts, Reginald Dwayne. "Only Once I Thought of Suicide." *Yale Law Journal* 125, January 15, 2016. https://www.yalelawjournal.org/forum/only-once-i-thought-about-suicide.

Betts, Reginald Dwayne. *A Question of Freedom*. New York: Penguin, 2010.

Betts, Reginald Dwayne. "We Must Give All Prisoners Access to Resources to Pursue College Education." *Time,* May 27, 2021. https://time.com/6052113/prisoners-college-education/.

Black By God: The West Virginian. https://blackbygod.org/.

Blackmon, Douglas. *Slavery By Another Name: The Re-Enslavement of Black Americans from the Civil War to World War II.* New York: Doubleday, 2008.

Blackwell, Christopher. "Reading While Incarcerated Saved Me. So Why Are Prisons Banning Books?" *New York Times.* August 17, 2022. https://www.nytimes.com/2022/08/17/opinion/banned-books-prison.html.

Blakinger, Keri, and Jolie McCullough. "Texas Prisons Stopped In-Person Visits and Limited Mail. Drugs Got In Anyway." *The Marshall Project.* March 29, 2021. https://www.themarshallproject.org/2021/03/29/texas-prisons-stopped-in-person-visits-and-limited-mail-drugs-got-in-anyway.

Boccio, Rachel. "Toward the Soul of a Transformational Praxis: Close Reading and the Liberationist Possibilities of Prison Education." *Pedagogy* 17, no. 3 (October 2017): 423–448.

Bradshaw, Elizabeth. "Tombstone Towns and Toxic Prisons: Prison Ecology and the Necessity of an Anti-Prison Environmental Movement." *Critical Criminology* 26 (2018): 407–422.

Brooks, Gwendolyn. *Blacks.* Chicago: Third World Press, 1987.

Brower, Jaime. *Correctional Officer Wellness and Safety Literature Review.* U.S. Department of Justice Office of Justice Programs Diagnostic Center. Washington, DC, 2013. https://s3.amazonaws.com/static.nicic.gov/Public/244831.pdf.

brown, adrienne maree. *Emergent Strategy: Shaping Change, Changing Worlds.* Chico, CA: AK Press, 2017.

Burton, Orisanmi. *Tip of the Spear: Black Radicalism, Prison Repression, and the Long Attica Revolt.* Berkeley: University of California Press, 2023.

Carson, E. Ann. "Mortality in State and Federal Prisons, 2001-2018—Statistical Tables." *U.S. Department of Justice.* April 2021. https://bjs.ojp.gov/content/pub/pdf/msfp0118st.pdf.

Carson, E. Ann. "Prisoners in 2019." *Bureau of Justice.* October 2020. https://bjs.ojp.gov/content/pub/pdf/p19.pdf.

Champion, Steve. "On Connection and Collaboration: Becoming a Writer in Prison."
　　Demands of the Dead: Executions, Activism, and Storytelling in the United States,
　　edited by Katy Ryan. Iowa City: University of Iowa Press, 2012, 59–73.

Chevigny, Bell Gale, ed. *Doing Time: 25 Years of Prison Writing.* New York: Arcade, 2011.

Clifton, Lucille. *Good Woman: Poems and A Memoir, 1969-1980.* Amherst: University of
　　Massachusetts Press, 1987.

Coogan, David, ed. *Writing Our Way Out: Memoirs from Jail.* Richmond: Brandylane,
　　2015.

The Correctional Leaders Association & The Arthur Liman Center for Public Interest
　　Law at Yale Law School. "Time-In-Cell: A 2021 Snapshot of Restrictive Housing
　　Based on a Nationwide Survey of U.S. Prison Systems." *Yale Law School.* August
　　24, 2022. https://law.yale.edu/centers-workshops/arthur-liman-center-public
　　-interest-law/liman-center-publications/time-cell-2021.

Davis, Angela Y. *Abolition Democracy: Beyond Empire, Prisons, and Torture.* New York:
　　Seven Stories, 2005.

Davis, Angela Y. *Are Prisons Obsolete?* New York: Seven Stories Press, 2003.

Davis, Angela Y., et al., ed. *If They Come in the Morning: Voices of Resistance.* New York:
　　Verso, 2016.

Davis, Angela Y., Gina Dent, Erica R. Meiners, and Beth E. Richie. *Abolition. Feminism.
　　Now.* Chicago: Haymarket, 2022.

Dear Books to Prisoners: Letters from the Incarcerated. New York: Left Bank Books, 2019.

Douglass, Frederick. *Narrative of the Life of Frederick Douglass: An American Slave,
　　Written by Himself*, edited by John R. McKivigan, Peter P. Hinks, and Heather L.
　　Kaufman. New Haven: Yale University Press, 2001.

Education Justice Project. "How Should We Measure Success in Prison Higher
　　Education Programs?" *Education Justice Project.* June 2021. https://education
　　justice.net/wp-content/uploads/2022/02/One_Pager_-_13_Higher_education
　　_programs.pdf.

Eliot, Leah. "The Types of Books We Cannot Send to Prisons (and Why)." *Appalachian Prison Book Project*. April 20, 2023. https://appalachianprisonbookproject .org/2023/04/20/the-types-of-books-we-cannot-send-to-prisons-and-why/.

Ellis, Eddie. "Open Letter Question of Language." *Center for NU Leadership on Urban Solutions*. May 21, 2020. https://perma.cc/JQ67-UKHZ.

Elsinore Bennu Think Tank. *Life Sentences: Writings from Inside an American Prison*. Cleveland: Belt Publishing, 2019.

Equal Justice Initiative. "Children in Adult Prison." *Equal Justice Initiative*. Accessed November 15, 2022. https://eji.org/issues/children-in-prison/.

Everett, Michael, and Lauren Woyczynski. "UCLA Law Releases New Database to Monitor Deaths in U.S. Prisons," *UCLA Covid Behind Bars*. Accessed May 2024. https://uclacovidbehindbars.org/intro-carceral-mortality.

Falkoff, Marc, ed. *Poems from Guantánamo*. Iowa City: University of Iowa Press, 2007.

Fathi, David. "Challenging Prison Reading Restrictions." *American Library Association Intellectual Freedom Blog*. September 28, 2021. https://www.oif.ala.org/oif/?p =26834&fbclid=IwAR2foqqVZ167xe3H2RDIALB7LksDy_NjvXqI8kIcsRKx3t Qdrgi3hUeDWW8.

Foner, Philip S. *Autobiographies of the Haymarket Anarchists*. New York: Humanities Press, 1969.

Franklin, H. Bruce, ed. *Prison Writing in 20th-Century America.* New York: Penguin, 1999.

Freedom to Learn Campaign. https://www.freedom-to-learn.net/.

Galloway, McKenna. "It's More than Just a Book: How the Appalachian Prison Book Project is Changing Lives One Page at a Time." *Times West Virginian*. June 10, 2023. https://www.timeswv.com/news/life/it-s-more-than-just-a-book-how -the-appalachian-prison-book-project-is-changing/article_db7c5550-061b-11ee -ba98-1b9a64e8cc44.html.

Garner, Jane. "'Almost like Freedom': Prison Libraries and Reading as Facilitators of Escape." *The Library Quarterly* 90, no. 1 (January 2020): 5–19. https://doi.org /10.1086/706309.

Gellman, Mneesha. *Education Behind the Wall: Why and How We Teach in Prison.* Waltham: Brandeis University Press, 2022.

Ghandnoosh, Nazgol, Emma Stammen, and Kevin Muhitch. "Parents in Prison." *The Sentencing Project.* November 17, 2021. https://www.sentencingproject.org /policy-brief/parents-in-prison/.

Gilmore, Ruth Wilson. "Forgotten Places and the Seeds of Grassroots Planning." *Engaging Contradictions: Theory, Politics, and Methods of Activist Scholarship,* edited by Charles R. Hale. Berkeley: University of California Press, 2008, 31–61.

Ginsburg, Rebecca, ed. *Critical Perspectives on Teaching In Prison: Students and Instructors on Pedagogy Behind the Wall.* New York: Routledge, 2019.

Gordon, Lisa, ed., *Contemporary Research and Analysis on the Children of Prisoners: Invisible Children.* Newcastle upon Tyne: Cambridge Scholars Publishing, 2018.

Gottschalk, Marie. *Caught: The Prison State and the Lockdown of American Politics.* Princeton: Princeton University Press, 2016.

Gottschalk, Marie. *Prison and the Gallows: The Politics of Mass Incarceration.* Cambridge: Cambridge University Press, 2006.

Gramsci, Antonio. *Letters from Prison,* edited and translated by Lynne Lawner. New York: Harper & Row, 1976.

Guenther, Lisa. *Solitary Confinement: Social Death and Its Afterlives.* Minneapolis: University of Minnesota Press, 2013.

Hager, Eli, and Anna Flagg. "How Incarcerated Parents are Losing Their Children Forever." *The Marshall Project.* December 2, 2018. https://www.themarshall project.org/2018/12/03/how-incarcerated-parents-are-losing-their-children -forever.

Hamade, Vanessa. "The First Page." *Appalachian Prison Book Project*. April 8, 2021. https://appalachianprisonbookproject.org/2021/04/08/the-first-page/.

Haney, Craig. "Mental Health Issues in Long-Term Solitary and 'Supermax' Confinement." *Crime & Delinquency* 49, no.1 (September 6, 2006): 124–56.

Harper, Destinee. "Found Between Pages: Volunteering with the Appalachian Prison Book Project." *Moveable Type,* no. 9 (January 2022): 1455. https://1455litarts.org/movable-type-issue-no-9-found-between-pages-by-destinee-harper/.

Harvey, Kendall. "Censorship in Prison Libraries: Danville and Beyond." *Illinois Library Association*. July 29, 2019. https://www.ila.org/publications/ila-reporter/article/118/censorship-in-prison-libraries-danville-and-beyond.

Hawthorne, Julian. *Subterranean Brotherhood* [1914]. Project Gutenberg, 2012. https://www.gutenberg.org/files/8406/8406-8.txt.

Hill, Joe. *The Letters of Joe Hill*, edited by Philip S. Foner. New York: Oak Publications, 1965.

Huling, Tracy. "Building a Prison Economy in Rural America." *Invisible Punishment: The Collateral Consequences of Mass Imprisonment*, edited by Marc Mauer and Meda Chesney-Lind. New York: The New Press, 2002, 197–213.

INCITE!, ed. *The Revolution Will Not Be Funded: Beyond the Non-Profit Industrial Complex*. Durham: Duke University Press, 2017.

Institute for Justice Research and Development. "The Economic Burden of Incarceration in the United States." *Florida State University*, 2016. https://ijrd.csw.fsu.edu/sites/g/files/upcbnu1766/files/media/images/publication_pdfs/Economic_Burden_of_Incarceration_IJRD072016_0_0.pdf.

Jackson, George. *Soledad, Brother: The Prison Letters of George Jackson*. Chicago: Lawrence Hill Books, 1994.

Jones, Carileigh. "Thoughts on Censorship and the Sociological Imagination in Prison." *Journal of Higher Education in Prison* 2, no. 1 (2023): 34–38. https://assets-global.website-files.com/5e3dd3cf0b4b54470c8b1be1/648e65d0712ee49319a8d194_JHEP_V2_Jones.pdf.

Kaba, Mariame. "A People's History of Prisons in the United States." *We Do This 'Til We Free Us: Abolitionist Organizing and Transforming Justice*. Chicago: Haymarket Books, 2021.

Kaba, Mariame. *We Do This 'Til We Free Us: Abolitionist Organizing and Transforming Justice*. Chicago: Haymarket, 2021.

Kaba, Mariame, and Kelly Hayes. *Let This Radicalize You: Organizing and the Revolution of Reciprocal Care*. Chicago: Haymarket, 2023.

Kaplan, Carol G. "Habeas Corpus: Federal Review of State Prisoner Petitions." *Bureau of Justice Statistics*. March 1, 1984. https://bjs.ojp.gov/library/publications/habeas-corpus-federal-review-state-prisoner-petitions.

Karpowitz, Daniel. *College in Prison: Reading in an Age of Mass Incarceration*. New Brunswick: Rutgers University Press, 2017.

Kelly, Emma. "Commentary: The Far-Reaching Effects of the Carceral State on Appalachian Communities." *100 Days in Appalachia*. August 10, 2021. https://www.100daysinappalachia.com/2021/08/commentary-the-far-reaching-effects-of-the-carceral-state-on-appalachian-communities/.

King, Jr., Martin Luther. "Letter from Birmingham Jail." *CSUChico*. Accessed May 2024. https://www.csuchico.edu/iege/_assets/documents/susi-letter-from-birmingham-jail.pdf.

Larson, Doran. *Fourth City: Essays from the Prison in America*. East Lansing: Michigan State University Press, 2014.

La Vigne, Nancy G. "The Cost of Keeping Prisoners Hundreds of Miles from Home." *Urban Institute*. February 3, 2014. https://www.urban.org/urban-wire/cost-keeping-prisoners-hundreds-miles-home.

Law, Victoria. *Resistance Behind Bars: The Struggles of Incarcerated Women*. Oakland: PM Press, 2009.

Lawson, John Howard, and Wesley Robert Wells. *Letters from the Death House.* Los Angeles: Civil Rights Congress, 1953.

Lazar, Steven. "'People Will Die': What It's Like to Be in Prison During the Coronavirus Pandemic." *Appalachian Prison Book Project*. April 27, 2020. https://appalachianprisonbookproject.org/2020/04/27/what-its-like-to-be-in-prison-during-the-coronavirus-pandemic.

LeFlouria, Talitha L. *Chained in Silence: Black Women and Convict Labor in the New South*. Chapel Hill: University of North Carolina Press, 2015.

Lennon, John J. "For Prisoners Like Me, Books are a Lifeline. Don't Cut It." *Guardian*. February 4, 2018. https://www.theguardian.com/commentisfree/2018/feb/04/for-prisoners-like-me-books-are-a-lifeline-dont-cut-it.

Lewis, David. *From Newgate to Dannemora: The Rise of the Penitentiary in New York, 1796-1848*. Ithaca: Cornell University Press, 1965.

Lim, Daniel. "Building Regenerative Cultures." *Daniel Lim Consulting*. May 2021. https://dlimconsulting.com/regenerativeculture/.

Litchfield, Kathrina Sarah. "A Critical Impasse: Literacy Practice in American Prisons and the Future of Transformative Reading." PhD dissertation, University of Iowa, 2014. https://doi.org/10.17077/etd.73bl2olb.

Lockard, Joe, and Sherry Rankins-Roberston, eds. *Prison Pedagogies: Learning and Teaching with Imprisoned Writers*. Syracuse: Syracuse University Press, 2018.

Love, Bettina. *We Want to Do More than Survive: Abolitionist Teaching and the Pursuit of Educational Freedom*. Boston: Beacon Press, 2019.

Malcolm X. *The Autobiography of Malcolm X*. New York: Ballantine, 2015.

Mandela, Nelson. *The Prison Letters of Nelson Mandela,* edited by Sahm Venter. New York: Liveright, 2019.

Marquis, Moira, and Dave "Mac" Marquis. *Books Beyond Bars: Stories from the Prison Books Movement*. Athens: University of Georgia Press, 2024.

McDonald, CeCe. "'Go Beyond Our Natural Selves': The Prison Letters of CeCe McDonald," edited by Omise'eke Natasha Tinsley. *Transgender Studies Quarterly* 4, no. 2 (May 2017): 243–65. https://doi.org/10.1215/23289252 -3815045.

Meeropol, Michael, ed. *The Rosenberg Letters*. New York: Routledge, 1994.

Meissner, Caits, ed. *The Sentences That Create Us: Crafting A Writer's Life in Prison.* Chicago: Haymarket, 2022.

Miller, Amy. "Appalachian Prison Book Project Fall 2019 Newsletter," *Appalachian Prison Book Project*. October 8, 2019. https://us7.campaign -archive.com/?u=80b64fbbab78210a17e1b27e0&id=82d928d766.

Montague, Maggie. "Books Make Time Move a Little Faster." *Appalachian Prison Book Project*. April 26, 2018. https://appalachianprisonbookproject .org/2018/04/26/books-make-time-move-a-little-faster/.

Mulvey-Roberts, Marie, ed. *Writing for Their Lives: Death Row U.S.A.* Urbana: University of Illinois Press, 2007.

National Academies of Sciences, Engineering, and Medicine. *Medications for Opioid Use Disorder Save Lives*. Washington, DC: The National Academies Press, 2019. https://doi.org/10.17226/25310.

National Alliance on Mental Illness. "Mental Health Treatment While Incarcerated." Accessed November 2022. https://www.nami.org/Advocacy/Policy-Priorities /Improving-Health/Mental-Health-Treatment-While-Incarcerated.

National Institute on Drug Abuse. "Drug Facts." Accessed November 2022. https://nida .nih.gov/publications/drugfacts/criminal-justice.

Nellis, Ashley. "The Color of Justice: Racial and Ethnic Disparity in State Prisons." *The Sentencing Project*. October 2021. https://www.sentencingproject.org/app/uploads/2022/08/The-Color-of-Justice-Racial-and-Ethnic-Disparity-in-State-Prisons.pdf.

Nickeas, Peter. "It's the Racial Stuff: Illinois Prison Banned, Removed Books on Black History and Empowerment from Inmate Education Program." *Chicago Tribune*. August 15, 2019. https://www.chicagotribune.com/news/ct-illinois-prison-books-removed-inmate-education-20190815-6xlrmfwmovdxnbc3ohvsx6edgu-story.html.

Ó Riain, Seán, and "Ray." *Condemned: Letters from Death Row*. Dublin: Liberties, 2008.

Oshinsky, David M. *"Worse than Slavery": Parchman Farm and the Ordeal of Jim Crow Justice*. New York: Free Press, 1996.

Patterson, Evelyn J., and Chris Wildeman. "Mass Imprisonment and the Life Course Revisited: Cumulative Years Lost to Incarceration for Working-Age White and Black Men." *Social Science Research* 53 (2015): 325–337.

Peltier, Leonard. *Prison Writings: My Life Is My Sundance*. New York: St. Martin's Press, 2016.

Perdue, Robert Todd, and Kenneth Sanchagrin. "Imprisoning Appalachia: The Socio-Economic Impacts of Prison Development." *Journal of Appalachian Studies* 22, no. 2 (October 2016): 210–23.

Pishotti, Gabriella. "Lessons From a Prison Book Club Volunteer." *Appalachian Prison Book Project*. January 8, 2020. https://appalachianprisonbookproject.org/2020/01/08/lessons-from-a-prison-book-club-volunteer/.

Porter, Lauren C., Meghan Kozlowski-Serra, and Hedwig Lee. "Proliferation or Adaptation? Differences Across Race and Sex in the Relationship Between Time Served in Prison and Mental Health Symptoms." *Social Science &*

Medicine 276 (May 2021). https://www.sciencedirect.com/science/article/abs/pii/S0277953621001477.

"Prison Letters Responds to Incarcerated People." *Yale Law School Today*. September 19, 2022. https://law.yale.edu/yls-today/news/prison-letters-project-responds-incarcerated-people.

Prison Letters Project. https://prisonlettersproject.org.

Pugh, Jordan. "We Will Be Here As Long As You Are Stuck There." *Appalachian Prison Book Project*. November 4, 2021. https://appalachianprisonbookproject.org/2021/11/04/we-will-be-here/.

Richie, Beth. *Arrested Justice: Black Women, Violence, and America's Prison Nation*. New York: New York University Press, 2012.

Roediger, Morgan. "What It Takes and What It Means." *Appalachian Prison Book Project*. July 16, 2021. https://appalachianprisonbookproject.org/2021/07/16/what-it-takes-what-it-means/.

Rosenberg, Ethel and Julius Rosenberg. *The Rosenberg Letters*, edited by Michael Meeropol. New York: Routledge, 2013.

Rubenstein, Batya Y. "Socioeconomic Barriers to Child Contact with Incarcerated Parents." *Justice Quarterly* 38, no. 4 (2021): 725–51.

Ryan, Hugh. *The Women's House of Detention: A Queer History of a Forgotten Prison*. New York: Bold Type Books, 2022.

Ryan, Katy, Valerie Surrett, and Rayna Momen. "Reading and Writing Between the Devil and the Deep Blue." *Teaching Literature and Writing in Prisons,* edited by Sheila Smith McCoy and Patrick Elliot Alexander. New York: Modern Language Association, 2023, 231–244.

Sacco, Nicola, and Bartolomeo Vanzetti. *The Letters of Sacco and Vanzetti,* edited by Marion Denman Frankfurter and Gardner Jackson. New York: Penguin, 1997.

Schept, Judah. *Coal, Cages, and Crisis: The Rise of the Prison Economy in Central Appalachia*. New York: New York University Press, 2022.

Schept, Judah, and Brett Story. "Against Punishment: Centering Work, Wages and Uneven Development in Mapping the Carceral State." *Social Justice* 45, no. 4 (2018): 7–34.

Sered, Danielle. *Until We Reckon: Violence, Mass Incarceration, and the Road to Repair.* New York: New Press, 2019.

Shakur, Assata. *Assata: An Autobiography*. Chicago: Lawrence Hill Books, 2001.

Simard, Suzanne. *Finding the Mother Tree: Discovering the Wisdom of the Forest.* New York: Knopf, 2021.

Smith, Caleb. Editor's Introduction to *The Life and the Adventures of a Haunted Convict*, by Austin Reed. New York: Modern Library, 2016, xv–lxii.

Solitary Watch. "FAQ: What is Solitary Confinement?" Revised June 2023. https://solitarywatch.org/facts/faq/.

Solomon, Akiba. "What Words We Use—and Avoid—When Covering People and Incarceration." *The Marshall Project*. April 12, 2021. https://www.themarshall project.org/2021/04/12/what-words-we-use-and-avoid-when-covering-people -and-incarceration.

Stanley, Eric A., and Nat Smith, eds. *Captive Genders: Trans Embodiment and the Prison Industrial Complex*. Oakland: AK Press, 2011.

Stern, Kaia. "Human Connection is Contraband. So How Do We Do Education?" *Journal of Higher Education in Prison* 1, no.1 (2021): 18–21.

Stevenson, Bryan. *Just Mercy: A Story of Justice and Redemption*. New York: One World, 2015.

Story, Brett. *Prison Land: Mapping Carceral Power Across Neoliberal America.* Minneapolis: University of Minnesota Press, 2019.

Surrett, Valerie. "The High Costs of Free Prison Tablet Programs." *Books Through Bars: Stories from the Prison Books Movement*, edited by Moira Marquis and Dave "Mac" Marquis. Athens: University of Georgia Press, 2024, 208–222.

Sweeney, Megan. *Reading Is My Window: Books and the Art of Reading in Women's Prisons*. Chapel Hill: University of North Carolina Press, 2010.

Szuberla, Nick, and Amelia Kirby, dirs. Up the Ridge. 2006; Whiteburg, KY: Appalshop. https://appalshop.org/shop/up-the-ridge.

Thompson, Heather Ann. *Blood in the Water: The Attica Prison Uprising of 1971 and Its Legacy*. New York: Pantheon Books, 2016.

Tager, James. "Literature Locked Up: How Prison Book Restriction Policies Constitute the Nation's Largest Book Ban." *PEN America*. September 2019. https://pen.org/wp-content/uploads/2019/09/literature-locked-up-report -9.24.19.pdf.

Toch, Hans. Foreword to *Prison Madness: The Mental Health Crisis Behind Bars and What We Must Do About It*, by Terry A. Kupers. San Francisco: Jossey-Bass, 1999, ix–xiv.

Vass, Kyle. "W.Va. Prisons Data Show Significant Racial Disparity in Recidivist Life Sentencing." *WV Public Broadcasting*. March 22, 2021.

Vasudevan, Shruthi. "A State by State Report: Letter Scanning Legislation in Appalachian Prisons and Jails." *Appalachian Prison Book Project*. April 26, 2023. https://appalachianprisonbookproject.org/2023/04/26/letter-scanning -legislation-in-appalachian-prisons-and-jails/.

Vera Institute of Justice. "Overdose Deaths and Jail Incarceration." Accessed December 2022. https://www.vera.org/publications/overdose-deaths-and-jail -incarceration/national-trends-and-racial-disparities.

Wagner, Peter, and Bernadette Rabuy. "Following the Money of Mass Incarceration." *Prison Policy Initiative*. January 25, 2017. https://www.prisonpolicy.org/reports /money.html.

Wagner, Peter, and Daniel Kopf. "The Racial Geography of Mass Incarceration."
    Prison Policy Initiative. July 2015. https://www.prisonpolicy.org/racial
    geography/report.html.

Wagner, Peter. "Why is West Virginia the Federal Prison Capital of the Country?"
    Prison Policy Initiative. June 10, 2014. https://www.prisonpolicy.org/blog/2014
    /06/10/wv-prison-capital/.

Waldman, Ayelet, and Robin Levi, eds. *Inside This Place, Not Of It: Narratives from
    Women's Prisons*. New York: Verso, 2017.

Wang, Leah, and Wendy Sawyer. "New Data: State Prisons Are Increasingly Deadly
    Places." *Prison Policy Initiative*. June 8, 2021. https://www.prisonpolicy.org
    /blog/2021/06/08/prison_mortality/.

Wang, Leah, Wendy Sawyer, Tiana Herring, and Emily Widra. "Beyond the Count:
    A Deep Dive into State Prison Populations." *Prison Policy Initiative*. April 2022.
    https://www.prisonpolicy.org/reports/beyondthecount.html.

Wang, Leah. "Prisons are a Daily Environmental Injustice." *Prison Policy Initiative*.
    April 20, 2022. https://www.prisonpolicy.org/blog/2022/04/20/environmental
    _injustice/?mibextid=Zxz2cZ.

Wang, Leah. "Research Roundup: The Positive Impacts of Family Contact for
    Incarcerated People and Their Families." *Prison Policy Initiative*. December 21,
    2021. https://www.prisonpolicy.org/blog/2021/12/21/family_contact/.

West, Charlotte. "They Saw the Demise of Pell. Now Federal Financial Aid is Coming
    Back." *Open Campus*. July 19, 2023. https://college-inside.beehiiv.com/p/saw
    -demise-pell-grants-now-federal-financial-aid-coming-back.

West Virginia Center for Budget and Policy. "The High Cost of Mass Incarceration in
    West Virginia." 2019. https://wvpolicy.org/wp-content/uploads/2019/02
    /WVCBP_IncarcerationInfographic_FINAL.pdf.

Wideman, John. *Brothers and Keepers*. New York: Mariner Books, 2005.

Widra, Emily. "Incarceration Shortens Life Expectancy." *Prison Policy Initiative*. June 26, 2017. https://www.prisonpolicy.org/blog/2017/06/26/life_expectancy/.

WVU Higher Education in Prison Newsletter. June 2023. https://higheredinprison.wvu.edu/news/newsletters/2023/08/03/vol-1-ed-1-2023-june.

RESOURCES

We compiled a non-exhaustive list of organizations that work to provide resources and knowledge. For a list of prison book projects, see the Prison Book Program's website: prisonbookprogram.org. We hope these resources are an inspiration to take action and spread the word about these projects and similar ones in your community.

Abolition-Aligned Initiatives

Abolitionist Law Center

"The Abolitionist Law Center is a public-interest law firm inspired by the struggle of political and politicized prisoners and organized for the purpose of abolishing class and race-based mass incarceration in the United States. Abolitionist Law Center litigates on behalf of people whose human rights have been violated in prison, educates the general public about the evils of mass incarceration, and works to develop a mass movement against the American punishment system by building alliances and nurturing solidarity across social divisions."

Appalshop Restorative Radio—Calls from Home

"Restorative Radio is rooted in Appalshop's nationally recognized Calls from Home program, which for more than a decade has sent messages and songs out over the radio from family members to their loved ones incarcerated in the mountains of central Appalachia. Calls from Home was created in response to aggressive state and federal initiatives to build prisons in the face of the declining coal industry."

Black and Pink

"Black & Pink National is a prison abolitionist organization dedicated to abolishing the criminal punishment system and liberating LGBTQIA2S+ people and people living with HIV/AIDS who are affected by that system through advocacy, support, and organizing."

Common Justice Initiative

"Common Justice develops and advances solutions to violence that transform the lives of those harmed and foster racial equity without relying on incarceration."

Critical Resistance

"Critical Resistance seeks to build an international movement to end the prison industrial complex (PIC) by challenging the belief that caging and controlling people makes us safe. We believe that basic necessities such as food, shelter, and freedom are what really make our communities secure. As such, our work is part of global struggles against inequality and powerlessness. The success of the movement requires that it reflect communities most affected by the PIC. Because we seek to abolish the PIC, we cannot support any work that extends its life or scope."

Prison Journalism Project: Independent Journalism by the Incarcerated

"Information about the prison system is limited, and policymakers and voters are shaping the lives of incarcerated people without their input. We're bringing transparency to the world of mass incarceration from the inside and training incarcerated writers to be journalists so they can participate in the dialogue about criminal legal reform."

Prison Radio

"An independent multimedia production studio producing content for radio, television, and films for 30 years and distributing throughout the world. We stream our high-quality audio material to media outlets and the general public in order to add the voices of people most impacted by the prison industrial complex."

Project NIA

"Project NIA—'nia,' meaning 'with purpose' in Swahili—is a grassroots organization that works to end the arrest, detention, and incarceration of children and young adults by promoting restorative and transformative justice practices."

Sentencing Project

"We advocate for effective and humane responses to crime that minimize imprisonment and criminalization of youth and adults by promoting racial, ethnic, economic, and gender justice."

Vera Institute

"Vera's mission is to end the overcriminalization and mass incarceration of people of color, immigrants, and people experiencing poverty. We pilot real-world programs developed with community members and the government. We incubate programs that will help end mass incarceration."

Resources for Reentry

All of Us or None

"All of Us or None is a grassroots civil and human rights organization fighting for the rights of formerly and currently incarcerated people and our families. We are fighting against the discrimination that people face every day because of arrest or conviction history. The goal of All of Us or None is to strengthen the voices of people most affected by mass incarceration and the growth of the prison-industrial complex. Through our grassroots organizing, we are building a powerful political movement to win full restoration of our human and civil rights."

Education Justice Project Reentry Guides

"EJP's Reentry Guide Initiative publishes three reentry guides, *Mapping Your Future: A Guide to Successful Reentry in Illinois*, *Mapping Your Future: National Edition*, and *A New Path: A Guide to the Challenges and Opportunities After Deportation*."

Fair Shake Reentry Resource Center

"Fair Shake is focused on the most important resource for reentry success: the person coming home. To this end, we provide free resources and information to incarcerated people, formerly incarcerated people, their friends and families, and other vital reentry stakeholders."

National Reentry Resource Center (NRRC)

"Funded and administered by the U.S. Department of Justice's (DOJ's) Office of Justice Programs (OJP), Bureau of Justice Assistance (BJA), the National Reentry Resource Center (NRRC) is the nation's primary source of information and guidance in reentry."

Project Rebound

"Project Rebound is a program that supports the higher education and successful reintegration of formerly incarcerated individuals wishing to enroll and succeed at California State University. By connecting students with critical resources, Project Rebound constructs an alternative to the revolving door policy of mass incarceration and increases community strength and safety.

Root & Rebound

"Root & Rebound restores power and resources to the families and communities most harmed by mass incarceration through legal advocacy, public education, policy reform, and litigation."

Resources for Incarcerated Individuals and Loved Ones

ACLU National Prison Project

"Through litigation, advocacy, and public education, we work to ensure that conditions of confinement are consistent with health, safety, and human dignity and that prisoners retain all rights of free persons that are not inconsistent with incarceration. Achieving these goals will result in a criminal justice system that respects individual rights and increases public safety for everyone, at greatly reduced fiscal cost."

Bar None

"Bar None is a volunteer-run, grassroots organization located in Humboldt County, California, that stands in solidarity with incarcerated people and their allies with the belief that prison abolition is a necessary part of building a future that is just, equitable, and empowering for everyone."

Center for Constitutional Rights

"The Center for Constitutional Rights is dedicated to advancing and protecting the rights guaranteed by the United States Constitution and the Universal Declaration of Human Rights. CCR is committed to the creative use of law as a positive force for social change."

Communities Not Cages

"Communities Not Cages is a grassroots campaign led by impacted people and families across New York State. Together, we are fighting to end mass incarceration and overhaul New York's racist and unjust sentencing laws."

Freedom Reads

"Freedom Reads is a first of its kind organization that inspires and confronts what prison does to the spirit. We bring beautiful, handcrafted bookcases into prisons, transforming cellblocks into Freedom Libraries. The library is a physical intervention into the landscape of plastic and steel and loneliness that characterizes incarceration. In an environment where the freedom to think, to contribute to a community, and even to dream about what is possible is too often curtailed, Freedom Reads reminds those inside that they have not been forgotten."

PEN America

"PEN America stands at the intersection of literature and human rights to protect free expression in the United States and worldwide. We champion the freedom to write, recognizing the power of the word to transform the world. Our mission is to unite writers and their allies to celebrate creative expression and defend the liberties that make it possible."

Prison Book Program National Prisoner Resource List

"This list provides information about places where people who are incarcerated and their families can find: support, advocacy, health care information (including HIV protection), outlets for their creativity, and lifelines to the outside community."

Solitary Watch

"Solitary Watch is a nonprofit watchdog organization that works to uncover the truth about solitary confinement and other harsh prison conditions in the United States by producing high-quality investigative journalism, accurate information, and authentic storytelling from both sides of prison walls. Solitary Watch's mission is to spur public debate and policy change on an underreported humanitarian crisis by promoting awareness, creating accountability, and shifting narratives."

West Virginia Family of Convicted People

"The West Virginia Family of Convicted People is a network of justice-impacted people who have come together to empower one another through advocacy and foster civic engagement in their community."

Resources for Higher Education in Prison

Alliance for Higher Education in Prison

"All people, regardless of whether they are currently or formerly incarcerated, should have access to high-quality and free higher education."

Formerly Incarcerated College Graduates Network

"We envision a society in which formerly incarcerated people of all races, genders, sexual orientations, and offense types pursue their dreams as educated and empowered citizens with valued experiences. We see a world in which we have the rights and opportunities needed to make important contributions to our communities and beyond."

Freedom to Learn Campaign

"Higher education in prison is more than a fight for scholarship, it is a fight for hope and humanity."

Prison Cells to PhD

"We are dedicated to promoting and advocating for higher education for currently and formerly incarcerated men and women. The UNLOCK Higher Ed Coalition is a group of stakeholders interested in policy solutions to increase educational access for individuals with criminal convictions."

ACKNOWLEDGMENTS

*T*hank you to the contributors for sharing their work. Reading, writing, and learning in prison and learning about prison go against the will of the institution; thank you for your resilience and for teaching those on the outside that enjoying a good story is a universal sanctuary. Thank you to everyone who writes to APBP, regardless of whether your work appears in this book, and to all the volunteers who respond to letters. Working with you brings so much joy.

Thank you to the APBP volunteers who helped make this book possible, with especial gratitude to Newport Benjamin, Erin Brock Carlson, Cari Carpenter, Jordan Carter, Vanessa Hamade, Karen Klein, Rayna Momen, Emily Ogden, Gabriella Pishotti, Beth Staley, Danielle Stoneberg, Madison Weaver, and many others who helped to collect quotes, send permissions, review drafts, edit the manuscript, and keep us on track. Thank you to Justin Schofield and Christine Titus for taking photographs of the artwork. Our great love to Dennis Allen and Darrin Lester who lifted all of us with their beautiful hearts and never stopped advocating for education and for justice.

Our gratitude to Steven Lazar who read the entire manuscript and provided thoughtful feedback. Working on this book has taught us the meaning of collaboration. Thank you for being our community.

Thank you to WVU Press for taking on this project and giving us a platform for this work.

Lastly, thank you to those struggling and fighting for freedom. Mariame Kaba is right: "Everything that is worthwhile is done with other people."[1] This struggle is worth it.

Note

1. Mariame Kaba, *We Do This 'Til We Free Us: Abolitionist Organizing and Transforming Justice* (Chicago: Haymarket Books, 2021), 178.

"I'd be lying if I said I knew where our finish line will be. We'll find out together."

—Craig Elias